John Edward Walsh

Rakes and Ruffians

THE UNDERWORLD
OF
GEORGIAN DUBLIN

FOUR COURTS PRESS

TECHNICAL AND LEGAL INFORMATION

This book was first published in Dublin in 1847 under the title *Ireland Sixty Years Ago*. It is reprinted from the third revised edition 1851; the preface and the last three chapters have been omitted. Subsequent typographically inferior editions were published under the titles *Ireland Ninety Years Ago* and *Ireland One Hundred and Twenty Years Ago*, the latter edition by Dillon Cosgrave (Dublin 1911), the author of *North Dublin: City and County* (Four Courts Press, 1977).

ISBN 0 906127 16 5   paperback edition
ISBN 0 906127 17 3   cased edition

This edition is published by Four Courts Press Limited, 3 Serpentine Avenue, Dublin and 4 and was printed in England by Billing & Sons Limited, Guildford.

CONTENTS.

John Edward Walsh

RAKES AND RUFFIANS: THE UNDERWORLD OF GEORGIAN DUBLIN

Here is a graphic account of the less sedate side of life in Georgian Ireland — a narrative which ranges from the gallows, bull-baiting, and feuds in the Liberties to duelling, abduction, carousing and gambling. John Walsh (1816-1869), a barrister, was Attorney-General for Ireland and Master of the Rolls. This book he published anonymously in the 1840s to show how things were before the Irish began to learn from the English about 'propriety and decency, peace and good order. . . .'

IRELAND SIXTY YEARS AGO.

CHAPTER I.

STATE OF SOCIETY AND THE CITY OF DUBLIN—LIBERTY BOYS
AND ORMOND BOYS—COLLEGIANS—POLICE—BUCKS AND
BULLIES—CHALKERS.

THE character of Ireland sixty or seventy years ago was an
anomaly in the moral world. Though united to England for
seven centuries, and every effort made during that period to
assimilate the people to its sober, prudent, and thinking neighbours, little progress seems to have been made in engrafting
their habits, manners, and modes of thinking, on the wild Irish
stock. The laws were promulgated, and sometimes enforced
with unrelenting severity ; yet there was no advance in the
general improvement of the people. Even within the pale, or
in the immediate vicinity of the metropolis, the king's writ was
nearly as much disregarded, in the eighteenth century, as when
Maguire of Fermanagh, in the sixteenth, demanded the price
of the sheriff's head, that if his people cut it off, his *Eric* might
be sent as a compensation to the Castle of Dublin. So little
change was made in the moral feeling of the nation, that laws
were inoperative. *Quid leges, sine moribus, proficiunt ?*

A characteristic sample of the spirit of the times is afforded
by the career of the well-known George Robert Fitzgerald,*

* See "FIGHTING FITZGERALD" (another volume of this series) for an account
of this extraordinary man.

B

in the strange and almost incompatible traits of character he displayed; his alternate gentleness and ferocity, love of justice, and violation of all law; his lenity and cruelty, patient endurance of wrong, yet perpetration of foul and atrocious murders. The scene of his outrages was, however, confined to a portion of Ireland separated from the rest by its local position on the remote shores of the Atlantic, seldom visited by strangers, having little intercourse with England, and either generally ignorant of its laws, or, from long impunity, setting them altogether at defiance. Still more striking are the examples of a kindred spirit existing among persons born and living within the pale of civilization, brought up among Ireland's best inhabitants, mixing with intelligent strangers, and having no excuse, from ignorance or seclusion, for violations of law and justice.

At the period we refer to, any approach to the habits of the industrious classes by an application to trade or business, or even a profession, was considered a degradation to a gentleman, and the upper orders of society affected a most rigid exclusiveness. There was, however, one most singular pursuit in which the highest and lowest seemed alike to participate with an astonishing relish, viz., fighting, which all classes in Ireland appear to have enjoyed with a keenness now hardly credible even to a native of Kentucky. The passion for brawls and quarrels was as rife in the metropolis as elsewhere, and led to scenes in Dublin, sixty or seventy years ago, which present a most extraordinary contrast to the state of society there at the present day.

Among the lower orders, a feud and deadly hostility had grown up between the Liberty boys, or tailors and weavers of the Coombe, and the Ormond boys, or butchers who lived in Ormond market, on Ormond quay, which caused frequent conflicts; and it is in the memory of many now living that the streets, and particularly the quays and bridges, were impassable in consequence of the battles of these parties. The weavers, descending from the upper regions beyond Thomas Street, poured down on their opponents below; they were opposed by the butchers, and a contest commenced on the quays which

extended from Essex to Island bridge. The shops were closed;
all business suspended; the sober and peaceable compelled to
keep their houses; and those whose occasions led them through
the streets where the belligerents were engaged were stopped,
while the war of stones and other missiles was carried on across
the river, and the bridges were taken and retaken by the
hostile parties. It will hardly be believed that for whole days
the intercourse of the city was interrupted by the feuds of
these factions. The few miserable watchmen, inefficient for
any purpose of protection, looked on in terror, and thought
themselves well acquitted of their duty if they escaped from
stick and stone. A friend of ours has told us, that he has gone
down to Essex bridge, when he has been informed that one of
those battles was raging, and stood quietly on the battlements
for a whole day looking at the combat, in which above a thousand men were engaged. At one time, the Ormond boys drove
those of the Liberty up to Thomas Street, where, rallying,
they repulsed their assailants, and drove them back as far as
the Broad-stone, while the bridges and quays were strewed
with the maimed and wounded. On May 11, 1790, one of
those frightful riots raged for an entire Saturday on Ormond
quay, the contending parties struggling for the mastery of the
bridge; and nightfall having separated them before the victory
was decided, the battle was renewed on the Monday following.
It was reported of Alderman Emerson, when Lord Mayor, on
one of those occasions, that he declined to interfere when
applied to, asserting that "it was as much as his life was
worth to go among them."

These feuds terminated sometimes in frightful excesses.
The butchers used their knives, not to stab their opponents,
but for a purpose then common in the barbarous state of Irish
society, to *hough* or cut the tendon of the leg, thereby rendering
the person incurably lame for life. On one occasion, after a
defeat of the Ormond boys, those of the Liberty retaliated in a
manner still more barbarous and revolting. They dragged the
persons they seized to their market, and, dislodging the meat
they found there, hooked the men by the jaws, and retired,
leaving the butchers hanging on their own stalls.

The spirit of the times led men of the highest grade and respectability to join with the dregs of the market in these outrages, entirely forgetful of the feelings of their order, then immeasurably more exclusive in their ideas of a gentleman than now; and the young aristocrat, who would have felt it an intolerable degradation to associate, or even be seen with an honest merchant, however respectable, with a singular inconsistency made a boast of his intimate acquaintance with the lawless excesses of butchers and coal-porters. The students of Trinity College were particularly prone to join in the affrays between the belligerents, and generally united their forces to those of the Liberty boys against the butchers. On one occasion several of them were seized by the latter, and, to the great terror of their friends, it was reported, they were hanged up in the stalls, in retaliation for the cruelty of the weavers. A party of watchmen sufficiently strong was at length collected by the authorities, and they proceeded to Ormond market; there they saw a frightful spectacle—a number of college lads in their gowns and caps hanging to the hooks. On examination, however, it was found that the butchers, pitying their youth and respecting their rank, had only hung them by the waistbands of their breeches, where they remained as helpless, indeed, as if they were suspended by the neck.

The gownsmen were then a formidable body, and, from a strong *esprit de corps*, were ready, on short notice, to issue forth in a mass to avenge any insult offered to an individual of their party who complained of it. They converted the keys of their rooms into formidable weapons. They procured them as large and heavy as possible, and slinging them in the sleeves or tails of their gowns, or pocket-handkerchiefs, gave with them mortal blows. Even the fellows participated in this *esprit de corps*. The interior of the college was considered a sanctuary for debtors; and woe to the unfortunate bailiff who violated its precincts. There stood, at that time, a wooden pump in the centre of the front court, to which delinquents in this way were dragged the moment they were detected, and all but smothered. One of the then fellows, Dr. Wilder, was a man of very eccentric habits, and possessed little of the gravity and decorum that distinguish the exemplary fellows of Trinity at the present day. He once met a young lady in one of the crossings, where she could not pass him without walking in the mud. He stopped opposite her; and, gazing for a moment on her face, he laid his hands on each side and kissed her. He then nodded familiarly at the astonished and offended girl, and saying, " Take that, miss, for being so handsome," stepped out of the way, and let her pass. He was going through the college courts on one occasion when a bailiff was under discipline; he pretended to interfere for the man, and called out—" Gentlemen, gentlemen, for the love of God, don't be so cruel as to *nail his ears* to the pump." The hint was immediately taken; a hammer and nails were sent for, and an ear was fastened with a tenpenny nail; the lads dispersed, and the wretched man remained for a considerable time bleeding, and shrieking with pain, before he was released.

Another striking instance of this laxity of discipline in the university occurred in the case of a printer of the name of Mills, He was publisher of the *Hibernian Journal*, and had incurred the anger of the students by some severe strictures on certain members of the college which appeared in his paper. On the 11th of February, 1775, some scholars drove in a coach to his door, and called him out on pretence of bargaining for some books. He was suddenly seized, thrust into the coach, and held down by the party within, with pistols to his head, and threats of being shot if he made any noise. In this way he was conveyed to the pump; and, after being nearly trampled to death, he was held there till he was almost suffocated—indeed he would have expired under the discipline, but for the prompt interference of some of the fellows. This gross outrage in the very courts, and under the fellows' eyes, which ought to have been visited by the immediate expulsion of all concerned, was noticed only by a mild admonition of the Board to a single individual; the rest enjoyed a perfect impunity, and openly exulted in the deed. The form of admonition actually excused the act. It was drawn up by the celebrated Dr. Leland, the historian of Ireland. It commenced in these words :—" Cum constet scholarium ignotorum cœtum injuriam admisisse in typographum quendam nomine Mills, qui nefariis flagitiis nobiliora quæque collegii membra in chartis suis lacessivit," &c.

The theatre was the scene of many outrages of the college students. One of them is on legal record, and presents a striking picture of the then state of society. On the evening of the 19th of January, 1746, a young man of the name of Kelly, a student of the university, entered the pit much intoxicated, and, climbing over the spikes of the orchestra, got upon the stage, from whence he made his way to the green-room, and insulted some of the females there in the most gross and indecent manner. As the play could not proceed from his interruption, he was taken away, and civilly conducted back to the pit; here he seized a basket of oranges, and amused himself with pelting the performers. Mr. Sheridan was then manager; and he was the particular object of his abuse and attack. He was suffered to retire with impunity, after interrupting the performance, and disturbing the whole house. Unsatisfied by this attack, he returned a few nights after with fifty of his associates, gownsmen and others. They rushed towards the stage, to which they made their way through the orchestra and across the lights. Here they drew their swords, and then marched into the dressing-rooms in search of Mr. Sheridan, to sacrifice him to their resentment. Not finding him, they thrust the points of their weapons through chests and clothes-presses, and every place where a man might be concealed,—and this they facetiously called *feeling* for him. He had fortunately escaped; but the party proceeded in a body to his house in Dorset Street, with the murderous determination of stabbing him, declaring, with the conspirator in *Venice Preserved*, " each man might kill his share." For several nights they assembled at the theatre, exciting riots, and acting scenes of the same kind, till the patience of the manager and the public was exhausted. He then, with spirit and determination, proceeded legally against them. Such was the ascendancy of rank, and the terror those " bucks " inspired, that the general opinion was, it would be impossible that any jury could find a *gentleman* guilty of an assault upon a *player*.

A barrister in court had remarked, with a sneer, that he had never seen a "gentleman player." "Then, sir," said Sheridan, "I hope you see one now." Kelly was found guilty of a violent assault, sentenced to pay a fine of five hundred pounds, and, to the surprise and dismay of all his gentlemen associates, sent to Newgate.

Sometimes students, in other respects most amiable, and on other occasions most gentle, were hurried into those outrages by the overruling spirit of the times, and a compliance with its barbarous usages. Among the lads at that time was a young man named M'Allister, whose fate excited as much pity as execration. He was a native of Waterford, and one of the young members of the university most distinguished for talent and conduct. He supped one night at a tavern, with a companion named Vandaleur; and they amused themselves by cutting their names on the table, with the motto, *quis separabit*. Issuing from thence in a state of ebriety, they quarrelled with a man in the street, and, having the points of their swords left bare through the ends of the scabbards (a custom then common with men inclined for a brawl), ran him through the body in the course of the fray. They were not personally recognised at the time; but the circumstance of carving their names on the table was adverted to, so they were discovered and pursued. M'Allister had gained his rooms in college, where he was speedily followed. He hastily concealed himself behind a surplice which was hanging against the wall, and his pursuers, entering the instant after, searched every spot except the one he had chosen for his superficial concealment. They tore open chests and clothes-presses, ran their swords through beds, but without finding him; and, supposing he had sought some other house of concealment, they departed. On their retreat, M'Allister fled on board a ship, and escaped to America, where he died. He was a young man of a most amiable disposition. Had he lived in better days, he might have been distinguished for gentleness and humanity; the spirit of the times and the force of example converted him into an atrocious murderer.*

* He was well known for his poetic talents. In his exile he wrote an elegiac epistle to his sister, to whom he was strongly attached; the strain of tender

Such riots and violence as we have described to have been frequent, seem hardly credible to those who know only our present well-ordered city and efficient police. But it is to be remembered that, at the period of which we write, there were no police. So keenly was the want of them felt, that, during the existence of the Volunteers, gentlemen of that body for a time arranged among themselves to traverse the streets at night, to protect the peaceably-disposed inhabitants, and men of the first rank in the kingdom thus voluntarily discharged the duties of watchmen. But the occupation assorted badly with the fiery spirits on whom it devolved, and the streets were soon again abandoned to their so-called legitimate guardians. In the day-time the streets were always wholly unprotected. The first appointment even of a permanent night-watch was in 1723, when an act was passed under which the different parishes were required to appoint "honest men and *good Protestants*" to be night-watches. The utter ineffi- ciency of the system must have been felt; and various improve- ments were, from time to time, attempted in it, every four or five years producing a new police act—with how little success every one can judge, who remembers the tattered somnambu-

affection it breathes, and the polished elegance of the versification, evince at once the taste of a cultivated mind and the feelings of a kind and warm heart. A few stanzas are here subjoined as a specimen :—

" Whilst thou, the chosen sister of my heart,
     With mirth dissembled, soothe a mother's woe,
Or solitary stray, and, scorning art,
     From genuine anguish give the tears to flow,
Behold thy brother, cruel Fortune's slave,
     With folded arms and brow depressed in care,
Where the beach bellows to the lashing wave,
     Indulge each mournful accent of despair.

   *   *   *   *   *

" Yet, torn from objects which my heart holds dear,
     Still shall my fondness for Eliza live :
Then take this prayer, accept a brother's tear,
     For prayers and tears are all I now can give—
' Parent of Nature, let thy sleepless eye
     Be ever watchful o'er Eliza's ways ;
Should stern misfortune threat, oh ! be Thou nigh,
     And guide her safe through life's intricate maze.' "

lists who represented the "good Protestant watchmen" a few years ago. Several attempts had also been made to establish an efficient civic magistracy, but with such small benefit that, until a comparatively recent period, a large portion of the magisterial duties within the city were performed by county magistrates, who had no legal authority whatever to act in them. An office was kept in the neighbourhood of Thomas-street by two gentlemen in the commission for the county, who made a yearly income by the fees; and the order to fire on the mob who murdered Lord Kilwarden, so late as 1803, was given by Mr. Bell, a magistrate of the county and not the city of Dublin. Another well-known member of the bench was Mr. Drury, who halted in his gait, and was called "the lame justice." On the occasion above mentioned, he retired for safety to the garret of his house in the Coombe, from whence, as Curran remarked, "he played with considerable effect on the rioters with a large telescope."

Among the gentry of the period was a class called "Bucks," whose whole enjoyment and the business of whose life seemed to consist in eccentricity and violence. Many of their names have come down to us. "Buck English," "Buck Sheehy," and various others, have left behind them traditionary anecdotes so repugnant to the conduct that marks the character of a gentleman of the present day, that we hardly believe they could have pretensions to be considered as belonging to the same class of society. These propensities were not confined to individuals, but extended through whole families. There was an instance in which one brother of a well-known race shot his friend, and another stabbed his coachman. They were distinguished by the appellatives of "Kilkelly" and "Killcoachy." At the same time, there were three noblemen, brothers, so notorious for their outrages, that they acquired singular names, as indicative of their characters. The first was the terror of every one who met him in public places—the second was seldom out of prison—and the third was lame, yet no whit disabled from his buckish achievements; they were universally known by the names of "Hellgate," "Newgate," and "Cripplegate."

Some of the Bucks associated together under the name of

the " Hell-fire Club ;" and among other infernal proceedings, it is reported that they set fire to the apartment in which they met, and endured the flames with incredible obstinacy, till they were forced out of the house ; in derision, as they asserted, of the threatened torments of a future state. On other occasions, in mockery of religion, they administered to one another the sacred rites of the church in a manner too indecent for description.   Others met under the appellation of " Mohawk," " Hawkabite," " Cherokee," and other Indian tribes, then noted for their cruelty and ferocity; and their actions would not disgrace their savage archetypes. Others were known by the soubriquet of "Sweaters and Pinkindindies." It was their practice to cut off a small portion of the scabbards of the swords which every one then wore, and prick or "pink" the persons with whom they quarrelled with the naked points, which were sufficiently protruded to inflict considerable pain, but not sufficient to cause death. When this was intended, a greater length of the blade was uncovered. Barbers at that time were essential persons to " Bucks" going to parties, as no man could then appear without his hair elaborately dressed and powdered. The disappointment of a barber was therefore a sentence of exclusion from a dinner, supper party, or ball, where a fashionable man might as well appear without his head as without powder and pomatum. When any unfortunate *friseur* disappointed, he was the particular object of their rage ; and more than one was, it is said, put to death by the long points, as a just punishment for his delinquency.

There was at that time a celebrated coffee-house, called " Lucas's," where the Royal Exchange now stands. This was frequented by the fashionable, who assumed an intolerable degree of insolence over all of less rank who frequented it. Here a Buck used to strut up and down with a long train to his morning gown; and if any person, in walking across the room, happened accidentally to tread upon it, his sword was drawn, and the man punished on the spot for his supposed insolence. On one occasion,—an old gentleman who witnessed the transaction informed us,—a plain man, of a genteel appearance, crossed the room for a newspaper, as one of the Bucks of

the day was passing, and touched the prohibited train accidentally with his foot. The sword of the owner was instantly
out, and, as every one then carried a sword, the offending man
also drew his, a small tuck, which he carried as an appendage
to dress, without at all intending or knowing how to use it.
Pressed upon by his ferocious antagonist, he was driven back
to the wall, to which the Buck was about to pin him. As the
latter drew back for the lunge, his terrified opponent, in an
impulse of self-preservation, sprung within his point, and
without aim or design pierced him through the body. The
Buck was notorious for his skill in fencing, and had killed or
wounded several adversaries. This opportune check was as
salutary in its effects at the coffee-house as the punishment of
Kelly was at the theatre.

On the 29th of July, 1784, six Bucks were returning home,
after dining with the Attorney-General, Fitzgibbon. As they
passed the house of a publican, named Flattery, on Ormond
quay, they determined to amuse themselves by "sweating,"
i. e., making him give up all his fire-arms. They entered the
house, and began the entertainment by "pinking" the waiter.
Mrs. Flattery, presuming on the protection that would be
afforded by her sex, came down to pacify them, but one of the
party, more heated with wine than the rest, assaulted and began
to take indecent liberties with her. Her husband, who had at
first kept himself concealed, in the hope that his tormentors
could be got quietly out of the house, roused by the insult to
his wife, rushed out and knocked the assailant down. The
Bucks drew their swords. Flattery armed himself with a gun,
and aided by the people of the house and some who came to
his assistance from the street, succeeded in driving them out on
the quay. The Bucks, who happened to hold high military
rank, unfortunately met with some soldiers, whom they ordered
to follow them, and returned to Flattery's house, vowing vengeance on all the inmates. A message had been sent to the
Sheriff, Smith, to come and keep the peace, but he was able to
collect only five men at the main guard, and when they reached
the scene of the riot, it was so violent that their assistance was
quite useless. The "spree" would probably have ended in the

total sacking of Flattery's house, only for the accidental arrival
of some gentlemen dispersing from a Volunteer meeting, who
willingly assisted the Sheriff. The "Bucks," however, escaped
being arrested. One of them was a noble lord, two were
colonels in the army, and the others of high rank and aides-de-
camps to the Lord Lieutenant, the Duke of Rutland. The
latter interested himself on their behalf; and such was the
influence of their rank, that the matter was hushed up, and the
gentlemen engaged in this atrocious outrage, though all well
known, escaped unpunished.

The excitement of these men was not, however, always of a
cruel or violent kind. Their eccentricities were often of a
peaceful character, and displayed themselves in a more harm-
less manner. Colonel St. Leger (pronounced Sallenger) was a
large man, handsome and well made, and particularly accept-
able to the society of the Castle during the viceroyalty of the
Duke of Rutland, and was a devoted admirer of the beautiful
Duchess, taking all occasions to display his gallantry, sometimes
in the most extravagant manner. Seeing her Grace wash her
hands and mouth one day after dinner, he called immediately
for the glass, and, standing up, drank to the bottom the contents. "St. Leger," said the Duke, "you are in luck; her
Grace washes her feet to-night, and you shall have another
goblet after supper."

The feat of another gentleman, who proposed a bet of a
considerable sum, that he would proceed to Jerusalem, play
ball against its walls, and return in a given time, is well known
in Dublin, and obtained the enterprising challenger a soubriquet by which he was ever afterwards universally known. His
name was "Whaley," and to the hour of his death, which
occurred recently, he was called "Jerusalem Whaley."

The legislature of the time presents a few striking illustra-
tions of the violent spirit exhibited in some of the anecdotes we
have here recorded. From 1773 to 1783 several acts were
passed enacting the most extreme penalties for the punishment
of offenders called "Chalkers." These acts recite that profli-
gate and ill-disposed persons were in the habit of mangling
others "merely with the wanton and wicked intent to disable

and disfigure them." They seem as appropriate to the gentlemanly brutalities of Bucks and Pinkindindies as to the feats of
their rivals the weavers and butchers, and there is an exception in the punishment, which seems adapted more particularly
for the former, viz., that while the punishment for "chalking"
is made in the highest degree severe, it is provided that the
offence shall not corrupt the offender's blood, or cause a for-
feiture of his property to the prejudice of his wife or relatives.
In 1783 the brutal custom of houghing (a favourite practice, as
we mentioned before, with the Dublin butchers in their feuds),
occasioned another statute, for the more effectual discovery and
prosecution of offenders called "Houghers." This latter act
had the curious effect of increasing the evil it was intended to
check. It adopted the clumsy contrivance of pensioning the
victim of the hougher for life on the district where the offence
was committed, unless the offender was convicted. It appears
from the act that the military were the class against whom the
practice of houghing was most in vogue, and when soldiers
became unwilling to continue in the army, either from being
employed against their political prejudices, or from being
entrapped as recruits, or from any other reason, they used
secretly to *hough themselves*, and, as the conviction of the
offender was then impossible, they thus obtained a pension for
life.

----◆----

CHAPTER II.

DUELLING—JUDICIAL AND LEGAL DUELLISTS—DUELLING CLUBS
AND RULES—HAYES—PAT POWER—BRYAN MAGUIRE—
TRIALS FOR DUELS.

THE universal practice of duelling, and the ideas entertained of
it, contributed not a little to the disturbed and ferocious state
of society we have been describing. No gentleman had taken
his proper station in life till he had "smelt powder," as it was
called; no barrister could go circuit till he had obtained a

reputation in this way; no election, and scarcely an assizes, passed without a number of duels; and many men of the bar, practising half a century ago, owed their eminence, not to powers of eloquence or to legal ability, but to a daring spirit and the number of duels they had fought. Some years since, a young friend, going to the bar, consulted the late Dr. Hodgkinson, Vice-Provost of Trinity College, then a very old man, as to the best course of study to pursue, and whether he should begin with Fearne or Chitty. The doctor, who had long been secluded from the world, and whose observation was beginning to fail, immediately reverted to the time when he had been himself a young barrister; and his advice was—"My young friend, practise four hours a day at Rigby's pistol gallery, and it will advance you to the woolsack faster than all the Fearnes and Chittys in the library." Sir Jonah Barrington gives some singular details illustrative of this, and a catalogue of barristers who killed their man, and judges who fought their way to the bench. We shall notice some of them, with a few additional particulars which Barrington has not mentioned.

Among the barristers most distinguished in this way was Bully Egan, Chairman of the Quarter Sesssions for the county of Dublin. He was a large, black, burly man, but of so soft and good-natured a disposition, that he was never known to pass a severe sentence on a criminal without blubbering in tears. Yet he, perhaps, fought more duels than any man on or off the bench. Though so tender-hearted in passing sentence on a criminal, he was remarkably firm in shooting a friend. He fought at Donnybrook with the Master of the Rolls, before a crowd of spectators, who were quite amused at the drollery of the scene. When his antagonist fired, he was walking coolly away, saying his honour was satisfied; but Egan called out he must have a shot at "his honour." On his returning to his place, Egan said he would not humour him, or be bothered with killing him, but he might either come and shake hands, or go to the devil. On another occasion he fought with Keller, a brother barrister. It was no unusual thing for two opposite counsel to fall out in court in discussing a legal point, retire to a neighbouring field to settle it with pistols, and then return to court to resume their business in a more peaceable manner. Such an instance occurred at the assizes of Waterford. Keller and Egan fell out on a point of law, and both retired from court. They crossed the river Suir in a ferry-boat, to gain the county of Kilkenny. Harry Hayden, a large man, and a justice of peace for the county, when he heard of it, hastened to the spot, and got in between them just as they were preparing to fire. They told him to get out of the way or they would shoot him, and then break every bone in his body. He declared his authority as a justice of the peace. They told him if he was St. Peter from heaven they would not mind him. They exchanged shots without effect, and then returned to court. The cause of their absence was generally understood, and they found the bench, jury, and spectators quietly expecting to hear which of them was killed.

Fitzgibbon, the Attorney-General, who was afterwards Lord Chancellor and Earl of Clare, fought with Curran, afterwards Master of the Rolls, with enormous pistols, twelve inches long.

Scott, afterwards Lord Chief Justice of the King's Bench and Earl of Clonmel, fought Lord Tyrawly on some affair about his wife, and afterwards with the Earl of Llandaff, about his sister, and with several others, on miscellaneous subjects, and with various weapons, swords, and pistols.

Metge, Baron of the Exchequer, fought with his own *brother-in-law*, and two other antagonists.

Patterson, Justice of the Common Pleas, fought three country gentlemen, and wounded them all; one of the duels was with small swords. Toler, Lord Norbury, Chief Justice of the Common Pleas, fought " fighting Fitzgerald," and several others. So distinguished was Mr. Toler for his deeds in this way, that he was always the man depended on by the administration to frighten a member of the opposition; and so rapid was his promotion in consequence, that it was said he *shot up* into preferment.

Grady, First Counsel to the Revenue, fought Maher and Campbell, two barristers, and several others *quos perscribere longum est.*

Curran, Master of the Rolls, was as much distinguished for his duels as his eloquence. He called out, among others, Lord Buckingham, Chief Secretary for Ireland, because he would not dismiss, at his dictation, a public officer.

The Right Honourable G. Ogle, a Privy Councillor, and member for Dublin, the great Orange champion, encountered Barny Coyle, a distiller of whiskey, because he was a papist; and Coyle challenged him, because he said "he would as soon break an oath as swallow a poached egg." The combatants were so inveterate, that they actually discharged *four* brace of pistols without effect. The seconds did not come off so well as the principals—one of them broke his arm by stumbling into a potato trench. Ogle was as distinguished a poet as a duellist, and his song of "Bannow's Banks" has been for half a century a prime favourite.

Sir Hardinge Gifford, Chief Justice of Ceylon, had an encounter with the unfortunate barrister, Bagnal Harvey, afterwards the rebel leader in the county of Wexford, by whom he was wounded.

The Right Honourable Henry Grattan, leader of the House of Commons, was ever ready to sustain with his pistols the force of his arguments. His cool ferocity, on such occasions, was a fearful display. He began by fighting Lord Earlsfort, and ended by shooting the Honourable Isaac Corry, Chancellor of the Exchequer. He called him, in the debate on the Union, "a dancing-master," and while the debate was going on, went from the house to fight him, and shot him through the arm.

So general was the practice, and so all-pervading was the duel mania, that the peaceful shades of our university could not escape it. Not only students adopted the practice, but the principal and fellows set the example. The Honourable J. Hely Hutchinson, the Provost, introduced, among other innovations on the quiet retreats of study, dancing and the fashionable arts. Among them was the noble science of defence, for which he wished to endow a professorship. He is represented in Pranceriana* as a fencing-master, trampling on Newton's

* "Pranceriana—a collection of fugitive pieces, published since the appointment of Provost Hutchinson, A.D. 1775."

Principia, while he makes a lunge. He set the example of duelling to his pupils, by challenging and fighting Doyle, a Master in Chancery; while his son, the Honourable Francis Hutchinson, Collector of the Customs in Dublin, not to degenerate from his father, fought a duel with Lord Mountnorris.

As if this was not a sufficient incentive to the students, the Honourable Patrick Duigenan, a Fellow and Tutor in Trinity College, challenged a barrister, and fought him; and not satisfied with setting one fighting example to his young class of pupils, he called out a second opponent to the field.

The public mind was in such a state of irritation from the period of 1780 to the time of the Union, that it was supposed three hundred remarkable duels were fought in Ireland during that interval. Counties or districts became distinguished for their dexterity at the weapons used—Galway, for the sword; Tipperary, Roscommon, and Sligo, for the pistol; Mayo for equal skill in both.

So universal and irrepressible was the propensity, that *duelling clubs* were actually established, the conditions of which were, that before a man was ballotted for he must sign a solemn declaration that he had exchanged a shot or thrust with some antagonist: and a code of laws and regulations were drawn up as a standard, to refer to on all points of honour. This was called, " The practice of duelling and points of honour settled at Clonmel summer assizes, 1755, by gentlemen delegates from Tipperary, Galway, &c., and presented for general adoption throughout Ireland." This singular national document is still extant, though happily now never appealed to.

The following occurrence, which took place in February, 1781, is characteristic of the mode in which points of honour were then settled. A gentleman in the uniform of the Roscommon Volunteers came into the room at a fashionable hazard-table. He was abused by one of the company present, with whom he happened to be engaged in litigation, and to whom, for that reason, he did not choose to reply. The bystanders imputing his silence to cowardice, added their sneers to the reproaches of his first assailant. One of the party, a subaltern in the army, was particularly severe in his taunts, and at

to length, in a paroxysm of indignation at what he conceived
be a disgrace to the military costume—being worn by a man
who appeared not to have a spark of courage—he came up to
the stranger, and rudely taking off his hat, tore the cockade
out of it, and threw it on the ground. The strange gentleman
drew his sword, and called upon any person who dared to come
forward till he would chastise him. The young officer declared
that he was under a promise never to fight in that house. The
parties therefore retired, but a hostile message was, of course,
immediately sent. The zealous subaltern, however, having
discovered that his antagonist, far from being a coward, was a
man of established courage and a skilful duellist, offered to
make any apology. None would be accepted which was not
as public as the insult, and the terms to which he was obliged
to submit were the following. He provided a cockade similar
to that he had taken from the gentleman's hat, brought it to
the coffee-room at the most public hour of the day, there in
presence of the company acknowledged his offence and asked
forgiveness, and taking his adversary's hat placed the cockade
in it, declaring he thought him most worthy to wear it.

Weapons of offence were generally kept at the inns, for the
accommodation of those who might come on an emergency un-
provided. In such cases "pistols were ordered for two, and
breakfast for one," as it might, and did sometimes, happen that
the other did not return to partake of it, being left dead on the
field. No place was free from these encounters : feuds were
cherished and offences often kept in memory till the parties
met, when swords were drawn, and the combat commenced in
the public street; a ring was formed round the parties, and
they fought within it like two pugilists at Moulsey Hurst. A
spectator described to us such an encounter which he witnessed
in St. Stephen's-green. One of the combatants was, we
believe, G. R. Fitzgerald. The parties were walking round
the enclosure in different directions, and as soon as they met
they sprang at each other like two game cocks; a crowd collected, and a ring was formed, when some humane person cried
out, " For God's sake, part them." " No," said a grave gentleman in the crowd, " let them fight it out ; one will probably be

killed, and the other hanged for the murder, and society will get rid of two pests." One of them did thrust the other through the tail of his coat, and he long exhibited in public, by his uneasy gait, the painful and disgraceful seat of the wound.

Among the duellists of the south of Ireland, at the close of the last century, were several whose deeds are still talked of. One was a gentleman named Hayes, and called " nosey," from a remarkable fleshy excrescence growing from the top of his nose, which increased to an enormous size. It was said to be the point at which his antagonist always aimed, as the most striking and conspicuous part of his person. On one occasion he tried in vain to bring an offender to the field, so he charged his son never to appear again in his presence till he brought with him the ear of his antagonist. In obedience to his father's commands, the son sought out the unfortunate man, seized him, and, as was currently reported, cut off his ear, and actually brought it back to his father, as a peace offering, in a handkerchief.

Another was Pat Power, of Daragle. He was a fat, robust man, much distinguished for his intemperance, and generally seen with a glowing red face. He on one occasion fought with a fire-eating companion called Bob Briscoe; when taking aim, he said he still had a friendship for him, and would show it; so he only shot off his whisker and the top of his ear. His pistol was always at the service of another who had less inclination to use his own; and when a friend of his declined a challenge, Power immediately took it up for him. When the Duke of Richmond was in the South of Ireland he knighted many persons, without much regard to their merit or claims. In Waterford he was particularly profuse of his honours in this way. Among his knights were the recorder, the paymaster of a regiment, and a lieutenant. Power was in a coffee-house conversing with a gentleman he accidentally met, and the topic of conversation was the new knights. He abused them all, but particularly " a fellow called B——, a beggarly half-pay lieutenant." The gentleman turned pale, and in confusion immediately left the coffee-room. " Do you know who that is?"

said a person present. "No," said Power; "I never saw him before." "That's Sir J. B—— whom you have been abusing." "In that case," said Power, with great unconcern, "I must look after my will." So he immediately proceeded to the office of T. Cooke, an eminent attorney, sat down upon a desk stool, and told him instantly to draw his will, as he had no time to lose. The will was drawn and executed, and then he was asked what was the cause of his hurry. He explained the circumstance, and said he expected to find a message at his house before him. "Never fear," said Cooke, the knight is an *Englishman*, and has too much sense to take notice of what you have said." Cooke prophesied truly.*

When travelling in England, Power had many encounters with persons who were attracted by his brogue and clumsy appearance. On one occasion a group of gentlemen were sitting in a box at one end of the room when he entered at the other. The representative of Irish manners at this time on the English stage, was a tissue of ignorance, blunders, and absurdities; and when a real Irishman appeared off the stage, he was always supposed to have the characteristics of his class, and so to be a fair butt for ridicule. When Power took his seat in the box, the waiter came to him with a gold watch, with a gentleman's compliments and a request to know what o'clock it was by it. Power took the watch, and then directed the waiter to let him know the person that sent it; he pointed out one of the group. Power rang the bell for his servant, and directed him to bring his pistols and follow him. He put them under his arm, and, with the watch in his hand, walked up to the box, and presenting the watch, begged to know to whom it belonged. When no one was willing to own it, he drew his own old silver one from his fob, and presented it to his servant, desiring him to keep it; and putting up the gold one, he gave his name and address, and assured the company he would keep it safe till called for. It never was claimed.

On another occasion he ordered supper, and while waiting

---

* A similar anecdote is told of a Mr. Bligh. It is probable that both he and Power, having acquired celebrity in the same line, may have been the heroes of similar achievements.

for it he read the newspaper. After some time the waiter laid two covered dishes on the table, and when Power examined their contents he found they were two dishes of smoking potatoes. He asked the waiter to whom he was indebted for such good fare, and he pointed to two gentlemen in the opposite box. Power desired his servant to attend him, and directing him in Irish what to do, quietly made his supper off the potatoes, to the great amusement of the Englishmen. Presently his servant appeared with two more covered dishes, one of which he laid down before his master, and the other before the persons in the opposite box. When the covers were removed there was found in each a loaded pistol. Power took up his and cocked it, telling one of the others to take up the second, assuring him "they were at a very proper distance for a close shot, and if one fell he was ready to give satisfaction to the other." The parties immediately rushed out without waiting for a second invitation, and with them several persons in the adjoining box. As they were all in too great a hurry to pay their reckoning, Power paid it for them along with his own.

Another of these distinguished duellists was a Mr. Crow Ryan. He shouted along the streets of Carrick-on-Suir, " who dare say boo," and whoever did dare say so, was called out to answer for it. The feats of another, the celebrated " fighting " Fitzgerald (mentioned at page 9), are still well remembered in Dublin. He made it a practice to stand in the middle of a narrow crossing in a dirty street, so that every passenger would be forced either to step into the mud, or jostle him in passing. If any had the boldness to choose the latter, he was immediately challenged.

The deeds of Bryan Maguire continued till a still more recent period " to fright the islanders from their propriety." He was a large burly man, with a bull neck and clumsy shoulders. His face, though not uncomely, was disfigured by enormous whiskers, and he assumed on all occasions a truculent and menacing aspect. He had been in the army serving abroad, and, it was said, dismissed the service. He availed himself of his military character, and appeared occasionally in the streets in a gaudy glittering uniform, armed with a sword, saying it was the uniform of his corps.   When thus accoutred he strolled through the streets, looking round on all that passed with a haughty contempt.   His ancestors were among the reguli of Ireland, and one of them was a distinguished Irish leader in 1641.   He therefore assumed the port and bearing which he thought became the son of an Irish king,   The streets were formerly more encumbered with dirt than they are now, and the only mode of passing from one side to the other was by a narrow crossing made through mud heaped up at each side.   It was Bryan's glory to take sole possession of one of those, and to be seen with his arms folded across his ample chest, stalking along in solitary magnificence.   Any unfortunate wayfarer who met him on the path was sure to be hurled into the heap of mud at one side of it.   The sight was generally attractive, and a crowd usually collected at one end of the path to gaze on him, or prudently wait till he had passed.

His domestic habits were in keeping with his manner abroad.   When he required the attendance of a servant he had a peculiar manner of ringing the bell.   His pistols always lay on the table beside him, and, instead of applying his hand to the bell-pull in the usual way, he took up a pistol and fired it at the handle of the bell, and continued firing till he hit it, and so caused the bell below to sound.   He was such an accurate shot with a pistol, that his wife was in the habit of holding a lighted candle for him, as a specimen of his skill, to snuff with a pistol bullet at so many paces' distance.   Another of his royal habits was the mode of passing his time.   He was seen for whole days leaning out of his window, and amusing himself with annoying the passengers.   When one went by whom he thought a fit subject, he threw down on him some rubbish or dirt, to attract his notice, and when the man looked up, he spit in his face.   If he made any expostulation Bryan crossed his arms, and presenting a pistol in each hand, invited him up to his room, declaring he would give him satisfaction there, and his choice of the pistols.   After a time Bryan disappeared from Dublin : he has since died, and has had no successor.

The laws by which duelling is punishable were then as severe as now ; but such was the spirit of the times, that they remained a dead letter. No prosecution ensued, or even if it did, no conviction would follow. Every man on the jury was himself probably a duellist, and would not find his brother guilty. After a fatal duel the judge would leave it as a question to the jury, whether there had been " any foul play ;" with a direction not to convict for murder if there had not. Instances have occurred within the last sixty years in which this question has gone to the jury.

The late Judge Mayne was a serious, solemn man, and a rigid moralist. His inflexible countenance on the bench imposed an unusual silence and sense of seriousness upon the court. A case of duelling came before him on the western circuit, accompanied by some unusual circumstances, which, in the disturbed state of the moral feeling of the time, were considered an alleviation. An acquittal was therefore expected as a thing of course. The judge, however, took a different view of the case ; he clearly laid it down as one of murder, and charged the jury to find such a verdict. His severity was a subject of universal reprobation, and his efforts to put down murder were considered acts of heartless cruelty. In a company of western gentlemen, when his conduct was talked over, some one inquired what was Judge Mayne's Christian name. " I cannot tell what it is," said another, " but I know what it is not—it is not *Hugh*." Since then a memorable change has come over the spirit of the times, and men, who had been slaves to public opinion, dared to brave it. Criminal informations for challenging or provoking to fight were ventured upon by gentlemen, even at the hazard of being considered cowards. In one term thirteen were filed from the neighbourhood of Galway. Duelling in Ireland, like drunkenness, is now nearly extinguished.

The mania seems to have commenced after the battle of the Boyne, and terminated with the Union. The effect of the first was, to disband a number of military men by the dissolution of the Irish army, who wandered about the country without employment or means of living, yet adhering with tenacity to the rank and feelings of gentlemen. They were naturally susceptible of slight or insult, and ready, on all occasions, to

resent them by an appeal to their familiar weapons—the sword
or pistol.   Their opponents, the Williamites, had been soldiers
likewise, and were not likely to treat with due respect ruined
and defeated men.   These causes, acting on temperaments
naturally hot and irritable, brought on constant collisions,
which were not confined to the parties, but soon extended
through all classes.   Since the Union, the sober and wiser
modes of thinking of our English neighbours have corrected
this, with others of our own unstable and more excitable habits.

CHAPTER III.

ABDUCTION—ABDUCTION CLUBS—THE MISSES KENNEDY—
MISS KNOX.

ABDUCTION, or forcibly carrying off heiresses, was another
of those crying evils which formerly afflicted Ireland ; but it
was an outrage so agreeable to the spirit of the times, and so
congenial to the ardent and romantic character of the natives,
that it was considered an achievement creditable to the man,
and a matter of boast and exultation to the woman.   From the
time that the King of Leinster abducted the frail Dervogle,
and royalty set an example of carrying off ladies, it was a constant practice.   When once it went abroad that a woman in
any station in life had money, she became the immediate object
of some enterprising fellow, who readily collected about him
adherents to assist in his attempt.   No gentleman or farmer
felt himself safe who had a daughter entitled to a fortune ; she
was sure to be carried off with or without her consent, and he
lived in a constant state of alarm till she was happily disposed
of in marriage.   It was generally the wildest, most " devil-
ma-care " fellow who undertook the enterprise, and unfortunately such a character was found to have most attractions in
the eyes of a young and romantic girl.

The frequency of this offence was such a crying grievance
that the legislature, at an early period, interfered to prevent it

and the law on this subject was made, and has since continued,* more stringent in Ireland than in England. So early as the year 1634 a statute had been passed for punishing such as "carried away maydens that be inheritors;" but this being found ineffectual, in 1707 *forcible* abduction was made a capital felony, and at the same time provisions were made for punishing those who carried off heiresses, though not forcibly, and preventing their ever enjoying their wife's property.† The law was however inoperative, from a notion which prevailed, that the offender was not punishable if the woman abducted him. The girl carried off was accordingly placed *before* the man on the horse, who thought he might thus evade the punishment; and the maidens so frequently, like the Sabines, became reconciled to their ravishers, that prosecutions bore a very small proportion to the number of offences.

A memorable instance of this occurred in a distinguished literary family in Ireland. Captain Edgeworth, a widower, with one son, married Mrs. Bridgeman, a widow, with one daughter. The young people formed an attachment for each other, at the early ages of fifteen and sixteen, and declared their love to their parents. The mother, however, was decidedly hostile to the match, and refused her consent. The young lady was an heiress, and the penalty of abducting her was known; so to avoid it she first mounted a horse, and assisted the young man to mount behind her. In this way she galloped off with her lover, and they proceeded to church and got married.

An association was formed in the south of Ireland, which could not have existed in any other country. This association was " an abduction club," the members of which bound them-

---

* These statutes, as well as those relating to chalkers, &c., which we before noticed, with the alterations made by subsequent acts, were all repealed in the consolidation of the criminal code in 1829; but the substance of the former was re-enacted. The capital punishment for forcible abduction has lately been ameliorated, as to offences after October, 1842.

† This latter act contains a curious clause, telling the story of one John O'Brien, who was a person of no property, and had forcibly carried off Margaret M'Namara, junior, who was entitled to two thousand pounds, and provides a special remedy for saving the two thousand pounds. The House of Commons would be not a little surprised at a private anecdote of this kind being introduced into a modern bill.

selves by an oath to assist in carrying off such young women as were fixed upon by any members. They had emissaries and confederates in every house, who communicated information of particulars—the extent of the girl's fortune, the state and circumstances of the family, with details of their intentions and domestic arrangements and movemeuts. When a girl was thus pointed out the members drew lots, but more generally tossed up for her, and immediate measures were taken to secure her for the fortunate man by all the rest. No class of society was exempt from their visits; and opulent farmers as well as the gentry were subject to these engagements of the clubs, according to their rank in life.

The persons who were most usually concerned in such clubs were a class of men abounding in Ireland, called "squireens." They were the younger sons or connections of respectable families, having little or no patrimony of their own, but who scorned to *demean* themselves by any *useful* or profitable pursuit. They are described by Arthur Young and other writers of the day, as distinguished in fairs and markets, races and assizes, by appearing in red waistcoats, lined with narrow lace or fur, tight leather breeches and top-boots, riding "a bit of blood," lent or given them from the stables of their opulent connections.

Hurling was at that time the universal amusement in which the gentry as well as the peasantry engaged, and in this athletic sport the squireens excelled. They were generally addicted to a base and brutal advantage sometimes taken in this noble exercise. It frequently happened, in pursuit of the ball, that two antagonists came into collision, and in the shock one of them, thrusting the handle of his hurley under his arm, took with the point of it his antagonist in the side, who in some instances fell dead, and in others remained with crushed ribs, a maimed and disabled man for life. This base act was not only practised, but applauded as a dexterous and justifiable *ruse.* On occasions when districts or counties challenged each other in this game, the rival parties were headed by the gentry of this class, who thus became identified with, and united to the peasantry.

These things, with a prestige in favour of family connexion or pretension to the rank of gentlemen, made young men of this class most popular and special favourites with the peasantry, who were ready and delighted to assist in any enterprise in which they were concerned. When a girl fell to the lot of a member of the club, it was probable he never had known or spoken to her, but it was his care to meet her at a public ball, where he generally contrived to make himself agreeable, and in the bustle and confusion of breaking up to put her into a chaise, or on horseback, with or without her consent.

Catharine and Anne Kennedy were the daughters of Richard Kennedy, of Rathmeadan, in the county of Waterford. Their father was dead, and they lived with their mother in much respectability; they were each entitled to a fortune, under their father's will, of two thousand pounds, a large sum at that time as a girl's portion in Ireland; but even that was exaggerated, and they were looked npon as co-heiresses of immense wealth, and, as such, were objects of great cupidity to the abduction clubs. The fortunate persons to whose lot they fell were Garrett Byrne, of Ballyaun, in the county of Carlow, and James Strange (pronounced Strang), of Ullard, in the county of Kilkenny. They were young men of great popularity in the country, dissipated, dashing, careless, spirited fellows, but of different dispositions. Strange was irritable, impetuous, and tyrannical, sacrificing everything to accomplish his ends, and little regarding the means or feelings of others. Byrne, on the contrary, was amiable, and, as far as his pursuits and propensities permitted, of a kind and gentle temper, particularly to women, with whom he was an universal favourite. He had attached himself to Catherine Kennedy, whose disposition was somewhat like, and congenial to his own. Strange had fixed his regards on Anne, who, in like manner, resembled him in determination and haughtiness of temper. In the intercourse of the country they had occasionally met at race-balls, and other convivial meetings, and the men had endeavoured to render themselves agreeable to the girls, with such success, that it was reported, on the authority of their confidential maids, that they were actually invited by them to avail themselves of the first opportunity to carry them off, as there were no hopes that their mother and friends would consent to their marrying men of such desperate fortunes.

While this intercourse was going on, Catherine was but fifteen, and her sister Anne but fourteen; they were both very lovely girls, but Anne was most distinguished, and her form and face gave promise of something eminently beautiful.

On the 14th of April, 1779, the girls accompanied their mother, aunt, and some friends, to a play enacted at Graigue-namana, a small town in the county of Kilkenny; and before the representation was concluded, a notice was conveyed to them that Byrne and Strange had formed a plan to carry them off that night from the play, and had assembled a number of adherents round the house for the purpose. In great alarm, the girls, with their mother and aunt, left the theatre, and retired to another room in the same house, accompanied by several gentlemen, their friends, who resolved to protect them. They bolted and barricaded the door, and remained for two hours without any attempt being made on the room. At length a violent rush was felt at it, the door gave way, and the party outside entered. There was a bed in the room, and the girls hastily retired behind the curtains, endeavouring to conceal themselves, and impress on the minds of the rioters that they had escaped from the apartment and were no longer in the house. For an hour or more the men seemed irresolute, and used no violence, but at the end of that time they rushed to the bed, and drew the girls from their concealment. They now displayed arms of all kinds, swords and pistols, with which they were provided, and in spite of all the opposition of the girls' friends, whom they fiercely attacked and threatened with instant death, they dragged them into the street, where they were surrounded by above one hundred armed men with shirts covering their clothes, by way of disguise, the then common costume, in which originated the name of "Whiteboys." Two horses were ready saddled. Catherine was forced to mount one, and placed before Byrne, and Anne was placed upon the other before Strange; and in this way, surrounded by a desperate body of men sufficient to intimidate and overawe the country, they were carried off from their friends. To allay the terrors of the the girls, it was proposed to send for other females who would be their companions. They received the proposal with joy, and they were speedily joined by some women, who proved, however, to be sisters and near relatives of the abductors, and prepared and in readiness to promote their criminal views.

They rode all night, surrounded by a strong armed guard of Whiteboys, to a place called Kilmashane, fifteen Irish miles from Graiguenamana. During the journey they were repeatedly solicited to consent to marry the men, and threatened that if they did not they should be carried to a distant country, where they never should see either mother or friends again. The women who had joined the party urged the same thing, and threatened if they persisted in their refusal, to abandon them, and leave them to whatever treatment the men chose to give them. In this place they obtained some refreshment, and continued for a considerable time subject to the constant importunity of the party. At length a man was introduced who was reported to be a priest, before whom Byrne and Strange took a solemn oath, that they would harrass them night and day, by riding through the country with them, till they should be exhausted with fatigue and suffering; but if they consented then to be married by the priest, they should be immediately restored to their friends. At length, terrified and subdued, they became passive, and a short form of ceremony was read, and an extorted assent was given. They then claimed the promise to be immediately restored to their friends, but it was evaded till night came on. The girls refused to retire to rest till solemnly assured by the females that one should sleep with each of them; they, however, abandoned them at midnight, and the men took their places.

From this house, which appeared to be a waste place and belonging to no master, they again were set on horseback as before, and, accompanied by their lawless patrol, they rode on to Borris, where they passed the next night. The exhausted girls entreated to be allowed to sleep with the females, but this was refused. After various wanderings, by riding night and day with a whole cavalcade of armed ruffians, they were brought to the house of another priest, who undertook to persuade them to submit to their fate, and be reconciled and obedient to their husbands. They still persisted in their remonstrances against the violence offered to them, when it was threatened to carry them to Castlecomer, and bury them there for ever in the coal-mines; and Strange, in a paroxysm of anger struck Anne in the face with a pewter pot. This brutal violence sunk deep into her mind, and rankled with an inextinguishable resent-ment never to be forgotten.

It will hardly be believed, that for *five weeks* they were paraded night and day, accompanied by their lawless caval-cade, and resting at miserable houses, through the counties of Waterford, Kilkenny, Carlow, Kildare, and so on to the north of Dublin, where they stopped at Rush, a small fishing town within a few miles of the metropolis. In this place they were put on board a vessel, accompanied by the whole party, and sailed to the town of Wicklow; where, with a feeling of per-fect indifference and security, some of the party went on shore; but while they were absent, the vessel was boarded by a Mr. Power, accompanied by an armed party, who rescued the harassed girls, and restored them to their friends. In the meantime Byrne and Strange made their escape to Wales; but they were instantly pursued, and were apprehended at Milford on the 6th of July, and lodged in the gaol of Carnarvon.

It was long doubtful whether they would not claim the girls as their wives, and a belief was entertained that no pro-secution would ensue. Catherine was said to be strongly at-tached to Byrne, who had always treated her with gentleness and affection, except in the manner of her abduction; but Anne's animosity to Strange was irreconcilable, and the brutal indignity of the blow was only to be effaced by his death. Though so young—a mere child—her energetic resentment overcame the reluctance of her elder but more yielding sister; her resolution was confirmed by a near relation of her own, distinguished by the number of duels he had fought, a Mr. Hayes, of whom we have before made honourable mention. It was by the unshaken determination of Hayes the men were brought to trial. The joint depositions of the girls were taken before the Lord Chief Justice Annaly, and Byrne and Strange were tried at the Kilkenny Lent assizes, on the 24th of March, 1780. Letters were produced from the young ladies, containing the most tender expressions of affection, and inviting their respective lovers to carry them off in the way usual in the country, to which they were ready and willing to consent. These letters, however, were clearly proved to be forgeries by the sister of Byrne, who was heard to boast she could perfectly copy Miss Anne Kennedy's handwriting. Others were read, really written by the girls, speaking of the men in an affectionate manner, and calling them their dear husbands, but these were proved to be dictated under the strong impressions of threats and terror. The men were found guilty, and sentenced to death.

It was supposed the sentence would never be executed. Their respectable rank in society—connected with all the gentry of the country—their actual marriage with the girls, and the frequency of the act of abduction, which made such a marriage be considered a thing divested of all criminality, created a strong feeling in their favour. The intercession of powerful friends, including, among others, the Minister from the Court of Vienna, was earnestly urged in their behalf. But Scott, afterwards Lord Clonmel, was then Attorney-General, and conducted the prosecution. He openly declared in court, that if this abduction was suffered to pass with impunity, there would be no safety for any girl, and no protection for the domestic peace and happiness of any family, and he called upon the government to carry out the sentence. His remonstrance was attended to, and the unfortunate gentlemen were hanged, to the great astonishment of their numerous friends and admirers. So strong and general was the excitement among the peasantry, that a rescue was greatly feared, and an extraordinarily large force of horse and foot was ordered to attend their execution ; and such was the deep sympathy for their fate, that all the shops were shut up, and all business suspended in Kilkenny and the neighbouring towns.

The subsequent fate of the girls was melancholy. Whenever they appeared in the towns of Waterford, Kilkenny, or the vicinity, they were assailed by hissing and hooting of the mob, who followed them with execration through the streets. They both had a pension from government, settled on them as a remuneration for their sufferings and their conviction of felons. This the common people considered as the price of blood, and could not conceal their abhorrence whenever they were seen. They were, however, respectably married. The eldest, Catherine, married a gentleman named Sullivan; but even he could not escape the superstitious credulity of the country. He was a worthy but weak man, and fancied himself haunted by the spectre of Byrne—frequently shouting out at night, when waking from a frightful dream, and declaring that he stood before him. He always kept a light burning in his room, as a protection against this apparition. His handsome wife fell into flesh, and preserved but little of that comeliness which attracted her lover, and she sought, it was said, the indulgence of smoking, to drown reflection! The fate of Anne was more severe. She fulfilled the promise of her youth, and became a dignified and magnificent beauty. She was married to a gentleman named Kelly. Her married state was miserable, and she died an object of great commiseration—sunk, it was said, in want and degradation. The common people declared her fate a judgment, and continued to execrate herself while living and her memory when dead. The very act of a man hazarding his life to carry her off was deemed a noble act, her prosecution a base return, and her misfortunes nothing but the vengeance of heaven visibly visited upon her.

Another awful catastrophe of this kind occurred in a different part of Ireland, about the same period, which is, perhaps, one of the most interesting and melancholy on record.

On the Derry side of the Foyle, and about two miles from the city, is Prehen, the seat of the Knoxes. It is highly wooded, and covers a considerable tract, descending to the river, and overhanging the broad expanse of water in this place with its dark shade. The circumstance which marked its ancient owners with affliction is of such a character as to correspond with the gloom that pervades its aspect; and no traveller passes it without many reflections on the sad event which happened there.

John M'Naghtan was a native of Derry. His father was an opulent merchant, and gave his son all the advantages of a most liberal education. He graduated in Trinity College, Dublin; but having inherited from his uncle a large estate, which precluded the necessity of engaging in any profession, he commenced a career of dissipation, then too common in Ireland. He married early, but his extravagance soon involved him in such distress, that he was arrested by the sheriff, in his own parlour, for a considerable debt, in the presence of his pregnant wife. The shock was fatal. She was seized with premature labour, and both wife and child perished. Being a man of address and ability, he was appointed to a lucrative situation in the revenue by the then Irish government, and in the course of his duty contracted an intimacy with the family of Mr. Knox, of Prehen, whose daughter, a lovely and amiable girl, was entitled to a large fortune, independent of her father. To her M'Naghtan paid assiduous court, and as she was too young at the time to marry, he obtained a promise from her to become his bride in two years. When the circumstance was made known to her father, he interdicted it in the most decided manner, and forbade M'Naghtan's visits to his house. This was represented as so injurious to M'Naghtan's character, that the good-natured old man was persuaded again to permit his intimacy with his family, under the express stipulation that he should think no more of his daughter. One day the lovers found themselves alone, with no companion but a little boy, when M'Naghtan took from his pocket a prayer-book, and read himself the marriage ceremony, prevailing on Miss Knox to answer the responses, which she did, adding to each, " provided my father consent." Of this ceremony M'Naghtan immediately availed himself; and, when he next met her at the house of a mutual friend, openly claimed her as his wife. Again he was forbidden the house by the indignant father. He then published an advertisement in all the newspapers, declaring the young lady was married to him. By a process, however, in the spiritual court, the pretended marriage was entirely set aside.

In the course of these proceedings M'Naghtan wrote a threatening letter to one of the judges of the court of delegates, and, it was said, lay in wait to have him murdered when he came on circuit, but fortunately missed him in consequence of the judges taking a different road. The result was, that M'Naghtan was obliged to fly to England. But here his whole mind was bent on obtaining possession of his wife; so at all hazards he returned, and lay concealed in the woods of Prehen. Warning of this circumstance had been communicated to her father, but he seemed to despise it. There was, however, a blacksmith, whose wife had nursed Miss Knox, and he, with the known attachment of such a connexion in Ireland, always followed his foster-daughter, as her protector, whenever she ventured abroad.

To detach his daughter from this unfortunate connexion, Mr. Knox resolved to leave the country, and introduce her to the society of the metropolis; and in the beginning of November, 1761, prepared to set out for Dublin. M'Naghtan and a party of his friends having intimation of his intention, repaired to a cabin a little distance from the road, with a sack full of fire-arms. From hence one of the party was dispatched to the house of an old woman who lived by the way-side, under the pretence of buying some yarn, to wait for the coming up of Mr. Knox's carriage. When it did arrive, the woman pointed it out, named the travellers it contained, and described the position in which they sat. They were Mr. Knox, his wife, his daughter, and a maid-servant. It was attended by but one servant, and the smith before mentioned. The scout immediately ran before, and communicated to M'Naghtan the information he had received. The carriage was instantly surrounded by him and three other men. M'Naghtan and one of his accomplices fired at the smith, whom they did not kill, but totally disabled. The blinds were now close drawn, that the persons inside might not be recognised. M'Naghtan rode up to it, and either by accident or design discharged a heavily-loaded blunderbuss into it at random. A shriek was heard inside. The blind was let down, and Mr. Knox discharged his pistol at the assassin. At the same moment another was fired from behind a stack of turf, by the servant who had concealed himself there. Both the shots took effect in the body of M'Naghtan. He was, however, held on his horse by his associates, who rode off with him. The carriage was then examined. Miss Knox was found dead, weltering in her blood. On the first alarm, she had thrown her arm about her father's neck, to protect him, and so received the contents of the murderer's fire-arms. Five balls of the blunderbuss had entered her body, leaving the other three persons in the carriage with her unhurt and untouched by this random shot.

The country was soon alarmed, and a reward of five hundred pounds offered for the apprehension of the murderers. A company of light horse scoured the district, and amongst other places were led to search the house of a farmer named Wenslow. The family denied all knowledge of M'Naghtan, and the party were leaving the house when the corporal said to one of his companions, in the hearing of a countryman who was digging potatoes, that the discoverer would be entitled to a reward of three hundred pounds. The countryman immediately pointed to a hay-loft, and the corporal running up a ladder, burst open the door, and discovered M'Naghtan lying in the hay. Notwithstanding his miserably wounded state, he made a desperate resistance, but was ultimately taken and lodged in Lifford gaol. Some of his accomplices were arrested soon after. They were tried before a special commission at Lifford, and one of them received as king's evidence. M'Naghtan was brought into court wrapped in a blanket, and laid on a table in the dock, not being able to support himself in any other position. Notwithstanding acute pain and exceeding debility, he defended himself with astonishing energy and acuteness. A singular trait of Irish feeling occurred in the course of the trial. One of his followers implicated in the outrage, named Dunlap, was a faithful and attached fellow, and his master evinced more anxiety to save his life than his own. As a means of doing so, he disclaimed all knowledge of his person: "Oh, master dear," said the poor fellow beside him in the dock, "is this the way you are going to disown me after all ?"

On the day of execution M'Naghtan was so weak as to be supported in the arms of attendants. He evinced the last testimony of his regard to the unfortunate young lady he had murdered, of whom he was passionately fond, and whom he mourned as his wife. The cap which covered his face was bound with black, his jacket was trimmed with black, having jet buttons, and he wore large black buckles in his shoes. When lifted up the ladder, he exerted all his remaining strength to throw himself off, and with such force that the rope broke, and he fell gasping to the ground. As he was a man of daring enterprise and profuse bounty, he was highly popular, and the crowd made a lane for him to escape, and attempted to assist him. He fiercely declined their aid, declaring, in a manner characteristic of the impetuous pride of his nature, that "he would not live to be pointed at as the half-hanged man." He called to his follower, Dunlap, for the rope which was round his neck, the knot of which was slipped and placed round his own. Again he was assisted up the ladder, and collecting all his energies, he flung himself off, and died without a struggle. His unfortunate but faithful follower stood by wringing his hands as he witnessed the sufferings of his dear master, and earnestly desired that his own execution might be hastened, that he might soon follow him and die by the same rope.

This murder and execution took place on the road between Strabane and Derry; and as the memory of them still lives among the peasantry, the spot is pointed out to passengers, and recalls traits of what Ireland was eighty years ago, even in the most civilized county. Abduction was then a common mode of courtship in the north, as well as the south, and a man was deemed a man of spirit if he so effected his marriage. Any fatal accident resulting to resisting friends was considered a venial offence, and the natural effect of their unreasonable obstinacy.

The circumstances and character of the parties in this affair rendered it one of the deepest interest. The young lady was but fifteen, gentle, accomplished, and beautiful, greatly attached to the unhappy man, devotedly fond of her father, and, with the strongest sense of rectitude and propriety, entangled in an unfortunate engagement from simplicity and inexperience.   The gentleman was thirty-eight, a man of the most engaging person, and a model of manly beauty.   His manners were soft, gentle, and insinuating, and his disposition naturally generous and humane; but when roused by strong excitement, his passions were most fierce and uncontrollable.   His efforts on his trial were not to preserve his life, which became a burden to him after the loss of her he loved, but to save from a like fate a faithful follower, and to exculpate his own memory from a charge of intended cruelty and deliberate murder.

CHAPTER IV.

CIVIC PROCESSIONS—RIDING THE FRANCHISES—THE LIBERTIES
—THE LORD MAYOR'S PENANCE.

THE greatest change wrought in any one body of our metropolis within the last century has decidedly been in our city corporation.   We speak not of the political alterations effected by " the act for transferring corporate abuses to other hands," as some one calls the corporation reform bill; but of a change of manners, as marked in the old corporation before its dissolution, as in its present successor—a change brought about, not by the operation of acts of Parliament, but by the silent progress of time and alteration of public feeling, and evincing itself in the almost total discontinuance of display in civic ceremonies and civic processions.   We have now no peregrinations of trades on their saints' days.   The shoemakers no longer perambulate with King Crispin at their head; and the smiths will never again walk in company with a limping Vulcan; nor the fishmongers' corporation personate the Twelve Apostles.   Even the very principal ceremony on which the boundaries of our civic liberties depended is no longer observed;

and though the Archbishop of Dublin were to depasture his horses on the Lord Mayor's garden, or the seneschal of St. Sepulchre's to execute an attachment under the very piazza of the post-office, the sturdy citizens will never again ride their franchises. The last miserable remnant of our corporate dignity is the Lord Mayor's annual procession, in his old glass coach, accompanied by a sorry troop of horse police; and the only merry-making that accompanies it is an occasional upset of that terror of pawnbrokers, the city marshal, from his military charger. Sixty years ago those things, though beginning to decline, had not wholly fallen from their ancient state; the remnant of them was kept up, and in some matters adhered to with as much earnestness as ever.

The principal civic ceremony which still continued within that period with unabated splendour was the triennial procession of the corporation, vulgarly called "riding the fringes." The great object of all civic corporations, in their original constitution, was the protection of the rights and properties of the citizens against the usurpation of powerful neighbours, church and lay, and the stout upholding of the several immunities and privileges conferred by their different charters. The vigilance of the Dubliners in ancient times, was principally to be exercised against their ecclesiastical neighbours of St. Mary's Abbey, Kilmainham, Thomas-court, and St. Sepulchre's, the latter being the liberty of the Archbishop of Dublin. Various were the disputes and feuds about their respective boundaries, and many are the charters and inquisitions defining them, which are still extant. To guard themselves from encroachment, the citizens from time immemorial perambulated the boundaries of their chartered district every third year, and this was termed "riding their franchises," corrupted into "riding the fringes." In ancient times, when the ecclesiastics were a powerful body, this was a very necessary ceremony, and in some measure a dangerous service. The worthy citizens went forth "well horsed, armed, and in good array;" and so they are described in an account of this ceremony in 1488, still extant in the book of Christ Church. But when the power and possessions of their clerical neighbours passed away, there was no one with the will or the means to interfere with them. The citizens had long ceased to march out with a black standard before them—"a great terror to the Irish enemies;" and their military spirit having completely died away, the riding of the franchises became altogether a peaceful exhibition of civic pomp, consisting chiefly of the following emblamatic personages, and display of craft :—

Every one of the twenty-five corporations was preceded by a large vehicle, drawn by the most splendid horses that could be bought or borrowed ; indeed all were eager to lend the best they had. On these carriages were borne the implements of the respective trades, at which the artisans worked as they advanced. The weavers fabricated ribbons of various gay colours, which were sent floating among the crowd ; the printers struck off hand bills, with songs and odes prepared for the occasion, which were also thrown about in the same manner ; the smiths blew their bellows, hammered on their anvils, and forged various implements ; and every corporation, as it passed, was seen in the exercise of its peculiar trade. They were accompanied by persons representing the various natures or personages of their crafts, mixing together saints and demigods, as they happened to be sacred or profane. Thus, the shoemakers had a person representing St. Crispin, with his last; the brewers, St. Andrew, with his cross; but the smiths, though patronised by St. Loy, were accompanied by Vulcan and Venus, which last was the handsomest woman that could be procured for the occasion, and the most gaily attired. She was attended by a Cupid, who shot numerous darts, *en passant*, at the ladies who crowded the windows. The merchants, who exist under the patronage of the Trinity, could not without profanation attempt any personal representation; but they exhibited a huge shamrock as the emblem furnished by St. Patrick himself, while they were also accompanied by a large ship on wheels navigated by *real* sailors.

The course of proceeding of this motley assembly was this : they drew up at the old custom-house, and passing along Temple-bar and Fleet-street, they came to the sea at Ringsend. They then proceeded to low-water mark, when a trumpet was

sounded, a water bailiff advanced, and, riding into the water as
far as he could, hurled a spear eastward. This marked the
eastern boundary of the city. They then crossed the Strand,
and traversing the boundaries of the city and county, by Merrion, Bray-road, Donnybrook, &c., came by Stephen's-green to
the division between the city and liberties. Then traversing
Kevin's-port, Bolton-lane, Bride-street, Bull-alley, &c., they
again emerged at Dolphin's-barn, from whence they took a
round by Stonybatter, Finglass, Glasnevin, and Clontarf, end-
ing a little beyond Raheny. In the course of this peregrina-
tion they passed through several houses, and threw down any
fences that came in their way, particularly on the confines of
the liberties.

The liberties of Dublin consist of an elevated tract on the
western side of the city, so called from certain privileges and
immunities conferred upon it. It contained formerly a population of forty thousand souls, who had obtained a high degree
of opulence by the establishment of the silk and woollen manufacture among them. After the Revocation of the Edict of
Nantz, a number of industrious artisans of the reformed faith,
driven from their own country, had taken refuge in this district, and brought the manufacture of silk and woollens to a
high state of perfection. About seventy years ago they had
three thousand four hundred looms in active employment; and
in 1791 there were twelve hundred silk looms alone. This
prosperity was liable to great fluctuations. Two years after,
when war was declared with France, and the raw material was
difficult to be procured, the poor artisans experienced great distress; but the breaking out of the insurrection in '98, in which
many of them were engaged, entirely ruined them; so that at
the time of the Union they were reduced to utter beggary.

On all occasions of distress, they descended in masses from
their elevated site to the lower parts of the town, and, as has
been remarked, they resembled an irruption of some foreign
horde—a certain wildness of aspect, with pallid faces and
squalid persons, seemed to mark, at these times, the poor arti-
zans of the Liberty as a separate class from the other inhabitants of Dublin. Of this famous and flourishing community

nothing remains at the present day but large houses, with stone fronts and architectural ornaments, in ruins, in remote and obscure streets; and a small branch of the poplin and tabinet manufacture, a fabric almost exclusively confined to them, and whose beauty and excellence are well known.

At the time of which we write, however, they exhibited their power on every public occasion; and during the perambulation of the Lord Mayor, they particularly signalized themselves. As they had manor-courts and seneschals of their own, with a court-house and a prison, they were exceedingly jealous of their separate jurisdiction. They assembled in detachments in some places leading to their territories, and made a show of strongly opposing any invasion of their independence. The most remarkable was on the Cross Poddle, leading to the Coombe, the great avenue to the interior of the Liberties; and here they made a most formidable exhibition of resistance. They seized upon the sword-bearer of the corporation, wrested from his hand the civic weapon, and having thus established their seeming right to resist encroachment, the sword was restored, on condition of receiving a present as a tribute, and liberating a prisoner from confinement. These demands being complied with, a formal permission was given to the procession to move on. The man who wrested the sword from the bearer had a distinguished name and an achievement to boast of during the rest of his life.

Besides hurling the spear into the sea, the Lord Mayor and Corporation observed several other ceremonies. In their progress they made various stops, and held sham consultations, which were called *courts*. At a court at Essex-gate it was a regular ceremony to summon Sir Michael Creagh in the following form :—" Sir Michael Creagh! Sir Michael Creagh! come and appear at the court of our lord the King, holden before the right honourable the Lord Mayor of the City of Dublin, or you will be outlawed." This singular ceremony originated from the circumstance of Sir Michael Creagh's having been Lord Mayor of Dublin in 1688, and absconded, carrying with him the gold collar of SS, which had been given to the Corporation only a few years before by Charles II. The civic citation to

the fugitive thief being wholly fruitless, and Sir Michael
Creagh never having returned with the collar, a new one was
obtained by Bartholomew Vanhomrigh from William III., in
1697, which is the one at present in use. The citation, however, continued to be made during the procession. The worthy
citizen through whom the collar of SS was restored was father
to Swift's celebrated Vanessa.

The trappings and equipments of this procession seem to
have been borrowed from the ancient practice of acting plays
or mysteries by the different guilds of the Corporation. Those
representations had been discontinued since the time of Elizabeth; they are, however, mentioned by many writers; and in
the books of the Corporation there are several entries relating
to the expenses, and mode of proceeding for them, which show
the allegories acted to have been similar to the characters
assumed by the guilds in riding the franchises. They were a
most extraordinary medley of religion and profanity, morals
and indecency. Thus, in the same interlude, the carpenters
acted the story of Joseph and Mary; the tailors, Adam and
Eve; while the vintners personated Bacchus and his companions, with their drunkenness and gallantries; and the
smiths, Vulcan and the intrigues of his fair consort; or, as it
was modestly entered, "Vulcan, and what related to him."
Such things formed regular items in the corporation accounts.
Several items are given in Whitelaw and Walsh's "History of
Dublin," and are sufficiently amusing. For a celebration of
St. George's day are the following:—

"Item 3. The elder master to find a maiden, well attired,
to lead the dragon; and the clerk of the market to find a
golden line for the dragon.

"Item 4. The elder warden to find for St. George four
trumpets; but St. George himself to pay them their wages."

On the subject of civic processions, we may mention one
which, though discontinued for many centuries, was much
talked of on the election of the first Roman Catholic Mayor of
the new corporation, viz., the ceremony of the Lord Mayor
walking barefooted through the city on Corpus Christi day.
The origin and account of this ceremony is given at length in

Stanihurst's " Chronicle." In 1514, there were constant disputes between Gerald Fitzgerald, Earl of Kildare, and James
Butler, Earl of Ormonde. The origin of the long-continued
feud between their two illustrious families is referred to the
contest between the houses of York and Lancaster; the family
of Kildare adhering to the house of York, and that of Ormonde
to the house of Lancaster. The government, after the accession
of Henry the Seventh, relied implicitly on the Kildare family,
and the Earl of Kildare was accordingly made deputy; but, in
the words of the historian, " James, Earl of Ormonde, a deepe
and farre reaching man, giving backe like a butting ram, to
strike the harder push, devised to inveigle his adversarie, by
submission and curtesie, being not then able to match him with
stoutnesse or pre-eminence. Whereupon Ormonde addressed
his letters to the deputie, specifying a slander raised on him
and his, that he purposed to defame his government, and to
withstand his authoritie; and for the cleering of himself and
his adherents, so it stood with the deputie his pleasure, he
would make his special repaire to Dublin, and there in an open
audience would purge himselfe of all such odious crimes, of
which he was wrongfullie suspected."

The Earl of Kildare having assented to this arrangement,
Ormonde marched to Dublin at the head of a " puissant army,"
and took up his quarters in Thomas-court, now a part of the
city, but then a suburb. The meeting was arranged to take
place in Patrick's Church. Before it took place, however, the
feuds between Ormonde's followers and the citizens had arisen
to an uncontrollable height; and during the conference, while
the leaders were wrangling in the church about their mutual
differences, their adherents came to blows, and a body of archers
and citizens rushed to the church, meaning to have murdered
Ormonde. The Earl, however, suspecting treachery, fled into
the chapter-house, and made fast the door. The disappointed
citizens, in their rage, shot their arrows at random through the
aisles and into the chancel, leaving some of them sticking in
the images. In the riot a citizen named Blambfeil was slain.

The Earl of Ormonde was so much alarmed that he would
not come out of his sanctuary till the deputy assured him of his

life by joining hands. A hole was accordingly cut in the door; but Ormonde, suspecting it was a trick to get an opportunity to chop off his hand, refused to put it out; so the Earl of Kildare, to reassure him, thrust his hand in, after which they shook hands, and were for the present reconciled. We give the result, so far as the citizens were concerned, in the historian's words :—

" Ormonde, bearing in mind the treacherie of the Dublinians, procured such as were the gravest prelates of his clergie to intimate to the court of Rome the heathenish riot of the citizens of Dublin in rushing into the church armed, polluting with slaughter the consecrated place, defacing the images, prostrating the relicks, rasing down altars, with barbarous outcries, more like miscreant Saracens than Christian Catholikes. Whereupon a legat was posted to Ireland, bending his course to Dublin, where, soone after, he was solemnly received by Walter Fitzsimon, Archbishop of Dublin, a grave prelat, for his lerning and wisdome chosen to be one of King Henrie the Seventh his chaplins, in which vocation he continued twelve yeares, and after was advanced to be Archbishop of Dublin. The legat, upon his arrival, indicted the city for this execrable offence; but at length, by the procurement as well of the Archbishop as of all the clergie, he was weighed to give the citizens absolution with this caveat, that in detestation of so horrible a fact, and *ad perpetuam rei memoriam*, the maior of Dublin should go barefooted through the citie, in open procession before the sacrament, on Corpus Christi daie, which penitent satisfaction was after in everie such procession dulie accomplished."

CHAPTER V.

DRUNKENNESS—NOTIONS OF CONVIVIALITY.

THE habit of intemperate drinking had grown to such an excess in Ireland, that it was gravely asserted there was some-

thing in the people's constitution congenial to the excitement
of ardent spirits.   The propensity of intoxication among the
people had been remarked from the earliest times. Sir W. Petty,
who wrote in the year 1682, when Dublin contained but 6,025
houses, states 1,200 of them were public houses, where intoxi-
cating liquors were sold.   In 1798, in Thomas-street, nearly
every third house was a public house.   The street contained
190 houses, and of these fifty-two were licensed to sell spirits.
Among the upper classes the great consumption was claret,
and so extensive was its importation, that, in the year 1763, it
amounted to 8000 tuns, and the bottles alone were estimated
at the value of £67,000.   This fact is detailed by honest Rutty,
the Quaker historian of the county of Dublin.   Such were the
convivial habits of the day, and so absorbed were the people in
the indulgence, that the doctor recommended that port should
be substituted in its place—" because," said he, with quaint
simplicity, " it would not admit so long a sitting—a great
advantage to wise men in saving a great deal of their precious
time."   In fact, the great end and aim of life in the upper
classes seemed to be convivial indulgence to excess.   The rule
of drinking was, that no man was allowed to leave the company
till he was unable to *stand*, and then he might depart if he
could *walk*.

If on any occasion a guest left the room, bits of paper were
dropped into his glass, intimating the number of rounds the
bottle had gone, and on his return he was obliged to swallow a
glass for each, under the penalty of so many glasses of salt
and water.   It was the practice of some to have decanters with
round bottoms, like a modern soda-water bottle, the only contrivance in which they could stand being at the head of the
table, before the host; stopping the bottle was thus rendered
impossible, and every one was obliged to fill his glass at once,
and pass the bottle to his neighbour, on peril of upsetting the
contents on the table.   A still more common practice was, to
knock the stems off the glasses with a knife, so that they must
be emptied as fast as they were filled, as they could not stand.
Sometimes the guests, as they sat down, put off their shoes,
which were taken out of the room, and the emptied bottles

were broken outside of the door, so that no one could pass out till the carouse was over.

Such orgies were not occasional, but often continued every night, and all night long. A usual exhortation from a father to his son was, "make you're head, boy, while you're young;" and certain knots of seasoned drinkers who had succeeded in this insane attempt, were called κατ' εξοχην, " the heads." from their impenetrability to the effects of liquor. It was said that, "no man who drank ever died, but many died learning to drink;" and the number of victims who fell in acting on this principle was an appalling proof of the extent of this practice —most families could point to some victim to this premature indulgence.

An elderly clergyman of our acquaintance, on leaving home, to enter college, stopped, on his way, at the hospitable mansion of a friend of his father for a few days. The whole time he was engaged with drinking parties every night, and assiduously plied with bumpers, till he sank under the table. In the morning he was, of course, deadly sick, but his host prescribed, " a hair of the old dog," that is, a glass of raw spirits. On one night he contrived to steal through a back window. As soon as he was missed, the cry of " stole away " was raised, and he was pursued, but effected his escape into the park. Here he found an Italian artist, who had also been of the company, but, unused to such scenes, had likewise fled from the orgies. They concealed themselves by lying down among the deer, and so passed the night. Towards morning they returned to the house, and were witnesses of an extraordinary procession. Such of the company as were still able to walk, had procured a flat backed car, on which they heaped the bodies of those who were insensible—then throwing a sheet over them, and illuminating them with candles, like an Irish wake, some taking the shafts of the car before, and others pushing behind, and all setting up the Irish cry, the *sensible* survivors left their departed insensible friends at their respective homes. The consequences of this debauch were several duels between the active and passive performers on the following day.

No class of society, even the gravest, was exempt from this indulgence. Even judges on the bench were seen inebriated, without much shame, and with little censure. One, well known, was noted for the maudling sensibility with which he passed sentence. It was remarked of him by Curran, that, " though he did not weep, he certainly had a drop in his eye." The indulgence was so universal, that pursuits of business never interfered with it. An attorney (Howard), writing in 1776, complaining of the want of reform in the law, and the evils of his profession, thus speaks:—" This leads me to mention an evil, which I would fain have thrown a veil over, but for the great degree of excess to which it has arrived in this kingdom, above all others, and even among the professors of the law, a profession which requires the clearest, coolest head a man can possibly have. Can we complain of being censured of dishonesty, if we undertake the management of a man's affairs, and render ourselves incapable of conducting them ? and is not this the case with every man who has filled himself with strong wines, unless he has such an uncommon capacity as not one in a thousand is ever blessed with ? The observation of Englishmen of business is, that they could not conceive how men in this kingdom transacted any business, for they seemed to do nothing but *walk the courts the whole morning, and devote the whole evening to the bottle.*"

Innumerable are the anecdotes which might be collected to illustrate the excessive indulgence in drink, now fortunately wholly exploded from all classes. Sir Jonah Barrington has recorded some, in which he was an actor, which are so highly characteristic, that we cite two of them, though, perhaps, already known to most of our readers. Near to the kennel of his father's hounds was built a small lodge; to this was rolled a hogshead of claret, a carcase of beef was hung up against the wall, a kind of ante-room was filled with straw, as a kennel for the company, when inclined to sleep, and all the windows were closed, to shut out the light of day. Here nine gentlemen, who excelled in various convivial qualities, were enclosed on a frosty St. Stephens day, accompanied by two pipers and a fiddler, with two couple of hounds, to join in the chorus raised by the guests. Among the sports introduced was a cock-fight, in which twelve game cocks were thrown on the floor, who fought together till only one remained alive, who was declared the victor. Thus, for seven days, the party were shut in, till the cow was declared cut up, and the claret on the stoop, when the last gallon was mulled with spices, and drank in tumblers to their next merry meeting. The same writer describes a party given in an unfinished room, the walls of which were recently plastered, and the mortar soft. At ten, on the following morning, some friends entered to pay a visit, and they found the company fast asleep, in various positions, some on chairs, and some on the floor among empty bottles, broken plates and dishes, bones and fragments of meat floated in claret, with a kennel of dogs devouring them. On the floor lay the piper, on his back, apparently dead, with the table-cloth thrown over him for a shroud, and six candles placed round him, burned down to the sockets. Two of the company had fallen asleep, with their heads close to the soft wall; the heat and light of the room, after eighteen hours' carousal, had caused the plaster to set and harden, so that the heads of the men were firmly incorporated with it. It was necessary, with considerable difficulty, to punch out the mass with an oyster-knife, giving much pain to the parties, by the loss of half their hair and a part of the scalp. Allowing all licence for the author's colouring, in what other country on the face of the earth could any thing like such scenes have occurred?

CHAPTER VI.

GAMBLING—LOTTERIES.

THE intense passion of the Irish for gambling has often been observed. Campion, writing nearly three hundred years ago, mentions it, and notices a class, called Carrowes, whose only occupation, all the year long, was playing at cards. He describes them as gambling away their mantles and all their clothes, and then lying down in their bare skins in straw by the road-side, to invite passers-by to play with them for their glibbes, their nails, their toes, and even more important parts of their bodies, which they lost or redeemed at the courtesy of the winner. Card-playing is, at this day, indulged in by the Irish peasantry with an eagerness perfectly astonishing, and is often the parent of many vices. It is not uncommon, in some places, to spend whole days playing for salt herrings; and as it is a point of honour to *eat* the stake, the player may suffer by losing, but a parching thirst is the only reward of winning The propensity for gambling exhibits itself at the earliest ages. Boys of ten years old, sent with car-loads of turf to market-towns, commonly gamble on the proceeds of their merchandize; and it is not unusual to see the young seller of a six-penny load beggar all his companions travelling the same road home.

This national propensity led to the most frightful excesses during the first government lotteries. Those very unwise and immoral devices for raising money were hot-beds for the growth of the passion in Dublin, where the humbler classes indulged in gambling with a frantic eagerness unknown in any other place. The mode which they adopted was what was called "insuring" a ticket; and it was even still more prompt and exciting than the purchase of one. An adventurer presented himself at the lottery-office during the days of drawing, and selected, among the undrawn tickets, a particular number, upon which he "insured"—*i. e.*, he laid a wager with the office-keeper that it would be drawn next day, or some particular day, or would be a blank or a prize, as the case might be. The risk was in proportion to the number of undrawn tickets; but it was so managed that the odds were usually silver to gold; thus, if five shillings were deposited, and the insurer won, he would get five guineas. These bets were made so low as a shilling, so that it was within the reach of every person to try his fortune. Lucky and unlucky numbers occupied the attention, and filled the minds of the citizens with omens and visions of success; a speculator walking the streets, if he acci-

dentally met an object he thought lucky, would run directly to
the lottery-office, and insure some number indicated by it;
when once the insurance was effected, it was not in the power
of the fascinated man to rest as long as his number remained in
the wheel; he went on increasing his premium while he had
any thing to pledge or sell.

The lottery-hall was in Capel-street, which was every day
choked up by the crowds of adventurers eager to hear their
fate.   The multitude of these unhappy beings, and the anxiety
and distraction they displayed, was sometimes appalling.   All
industry was suspended; a number was to be insured at any
risk, though the means were secured by pawning, selling, or
robbery; every faculty seemed absorbed in watching the chance
of the number when procured; all the excesses that have been
attributed to gambling in a few of the upper classes, were here
displayed by the whole population; the scenes that shock an
observer in the privacy of a gaming-house were of common
occurrence in the public streets—the cheer of success and the
groan of ruin, the wildness of exultation and the frenzy of
despair, were daily to be witnessed.   The man who was
honest before became a thief, that he might have the means of
insuring.   The very beggars allocated their alms to this fasci-
nating pursuit.   A poor blind creature used to beg in Sack-
ville-street, and attracted the notice of passengers by her silent
and unobtrusive manners and cleanly appearance.   She had a
little basket with articles for sale, covered with a net, and
received more alms than an ordinary beggar.   She dreamed of
a number that was to make her fortune ; and next day was led
to a lottery-office, and insured it.   It was not drawn, and she
lost; but convinced that it was to make her fortune she still
persevered in insuring it.   Her little store was soon exhausted ;
she sold her clothes, and pledged her basket; but her number
still stuck in the wheel, and when she had nothing left she
was obliged to desist.   She still, however, inquired after the
number, and found it had been drawn the very day she ceased
to insure it.   She groped her way to the Royal Canal, and
threw herself into it.

The hall in which the drawings took place was open to the

public.   Two large wheels were set on a slope, beside which stood two boys of the Blue Coat Hospital, each with one hand thrust into his belt behind his back, and the other flourishing in the air; on every turn of the wheels they dived in and took a rolled-up packet from each, one containing a number, and the other a blank or prize ; one clerk then read the number aloud, and another declared its fate.   This hall was usually crowded with persons anxious to know their own or their friends' fortunes.   So absorbing was the interest connected with every thing belonging to the lottery, that it is said an impostor made a considerable sum of money by exhibiting himself, for a shilling admittance, in Capel-street, as the person who got a £20,000 prize.

The misery and vice caused by this species of gambling evoked some strong remonstrances, and many memorials to government; but the ministers of the day were reluctant to forego the trifling advantage of a loan without interest, for the short period for which a lottery procured it—the only benefit derived from this demoralizing device.   The practices above described were, however, prohibited by the legislature, and the insurance of tickets made penal in 1793; and several wholesome regulations and restrictions were introduced, which very much ameliorated and modified the evils of subsequent state lotteries.

CHAPTER VII.

SHOEBLACKS—THE STREETS—PUBLIC VEHICLES.

THE common people of Dublin were eminently distinguished by peculiar traits of character, in which they differed from the populace of every other city.   Among them, the shoeblacks were a numerous and formidable body, the precursors of Day and Martin, till the superior merits of the latter put an end to the trade.   The polish they used was lampblack and eggs, of which they purchased in the markets all that were rotten.

Their implements consisted of a three-legged stool, a basket containing a blunt knife, called a spudd, a painter's brush, and an old wig. A gentleman going out in the morning with dirty boots or shoes, was sure to find a shoeblack sitting on his stool at the corner of the street. He laid his foot in his lap without ceremony, where the artist scraped it with his spudd, wiped it with his wig, and then laid on his composition as thick as black paint with his painter's brush. The stuff dried with a rich polish, requiring no friction, and little inferior to the elaborated modern fluids, save only in the intolerable odour exhaled from eggs in a high state of putridity, and which filled any house you entered before the composition was quite dry, and sometimes tainted even the air of fashionable drawing-rooms. Polishing shoes, we should mention, was at this time a refinement almost confined to cities, people in the country being generally satisfied with grease. The circumstance is recorded in the ballad of the famous wedding of Baltimore :

"Oh ! lay by the fat to grease the priest's boots."

Goose grease was the favourite and most fashionable, and so was reserved for his reverence.

These artists were distinguished for other qualities as well as professional skill. Their costume was singularly squalid— if possible, generally exceeding the representation of the brother of the brush preserved in Hogarth's picture of the idle apprentice, one of whose associates is a member of the craft, with his basket and brush, playing chuck-farthing on a tombstone during divine service on Sunday. But the Dublin shoeblack far excelled his English contemporary in qualities designated by the alliteration of " wit and wickedness, dirt and drollery." Miss Edgeworth has preserved some traits of their genius in her admirable essay on Irish bulls, most ingeniously proving that what appeared to be the blundering phraseology of this class was in reality figurative and poetical language, and a tissue of tropes and metaphors.*

* The sketch is so generally known, that we forbear to quote it. The fair authoress will pardon us, however, if we suggest an amendment. In her version, Bill concludes his statement with the following passage : — " You lie,

One known by the simple appellation of "Bill,"—perhaps the very Bill whom Miss Edgeworth has immortalized,—was distinguished on many other occasions for his ready wit. He generally sat on Ormond Quay, at the corner of Arran Street, and had an overflow of customers, who resorted to his stool, as much to hear his wit as to receive his polish.   Some ladies, at that time stars in the Irish court, were not very scrupulous in seeking such entertainment, and frequently accosted Bill to hear his *bon mots*, though they were not always fit to be repeated.

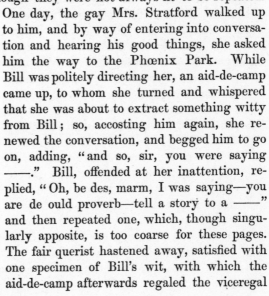

One day, the gay Mrs. Stratford walked up to him, and by way of entering into conversation and hearing his good things, she asked him the way to the Phœnix Park.   While Bill was politely directing her, an aid-de-camp came up, to whom she turned and whispered that she was about to extract something witty from Bill; so, accosting him again, she renewed the conversation, and begged him to go on, adding, "and so, sir, you were saying ——."   Bill, offended at her inattention, replied, "Oh, be des, marm, I was saying—you are de ould proverb—tell a story to a ——" and then repeated one, which, though singularly apposite, is too coarse for these pages. The fair querist hastened away, satisfied with one specimen of Bill's wit, with which the aid-de-camp afterwards regaled the viceregal

says I; with that, he ups with a lump of a two-year old, and lets drive at me. I outs with my bread-earner, and gives it him up to Lamprey in the bread-basket." All the knives were then made by the famous cutler of the name of Lamprey, which was impressed on the blade. The true reading is, "up to de Y in the bread-basket," the name being always formed with the L to the point and the Y to the handle; so that not only the blade, but the very name, to the last letter, was buried in his body. This was literally the classical description quoted by Miss Edgeworth— *capulo tenus abdidit ensem.* We give a sketch of this now extinct instrument: an inspection of it will give an idea of the singular force of the expression.

circle. Such coarse humour was the delight of the court then held in the castle of Dublin.

The number of crippled and deformed beggars that even to the present day haunt all places of resort in Ireland, has long been a subject of remark to strangers. Among the notable efforts of the Irish parliament for the relief of the poor, was one of turning this class, the maimed and halt, in Dublin, into shoe-blacks and newsvenders. To secure them employment, a statute was passed in 1773, by which young and able-bodied shoeblacks, in the city, were made liable to be committed as vagabonds. This provision, like many others of the very silly code of which it formed a part, seems never to have been very rigidly executed; and for many a year afterwards the frater-nity flourished as sound in health and limb as ever.

The rapid improvement of the streets was destined, how-ever, soon to prove far more destructive to the craft than com-mitments; and Messrs. MacAdam and the paving-board were worse enemies than beadles and parish constables. The state of the best streets, about a century ago, was much worse than the Pill Lane or Goat Alley of 1847. There were no areas in front of houses, as there are now in all streets consisting of private residences; and the spouts, instead of being carried down to the ground by trunks, so as to suffer the water to run off in a confined stream, projected out either from the roof, or half-way down the wall, so as to pour in torrents over a large space below, after every shower. Sewers there were few or none, and many houses having no rere or place of deposit behind, the inhabitants threw all species of filth into the middle of the street, so that Dublin was as little purified as Edinburgh or Lisbon. As late as the year 1811 there was not one covered sewer in the most populous district of the city—the Liberty, south of the Coombe; and it is a very singular circumstance, that when the great sewer through Capel Street was commenced under the powers vested in the paving-board, after 1806, that street being then one of the most populous in Dublin, and in which the most thriving shopkeepers of the day lived, the sewer was covered in at *the desire of the inhabitants*, and left unfinished.*

* "History of Dublin," vol. ii. p. 1077. The sewer was so wide and deep in

For want of sewers, the filth and water were received in pits, called cesspools, dug before the doors, and covered in; and those continued in Sackville Street, and other places, long after the year 1810; and many now remember the horrid sight and smell which periodically offended the inhabitants in the most fashionable streets, when those stygian pools were opened and emptied.

To the causes of accumulating filth was to be added the excessive narrowness of the streets. Chancery Lane, once one of the most fashionable streets in the city, and the residence of all the leading members of the legal profession, who have now migrated to Merrion Square, is hardly the width of a modern stable-lane; and Cutpurse Row, the leading thoroughfare from the southern road to the eastern end of the town was, before it was widened, in 1810, only fifteen feet broad.

Among the momentos of the former state of the streets of our metropolis, some, not the least curious, are the various acts passed for their improvement, which draw most piteous pictures of their condition. From one passed in 1717 it appears to have been a lucrative bnsiness to lay dirt in the streets for the purpose of making manure. In such a state of the city shoeblacks must have had a thriving trade. The face of things is now changed. Dublin is one of the cleanest cities in Europe, and a pedestrian may walk from east to west and north to south of it without soiling his foot.

The advance of this improvement in our metropolis was occasionally marked by events which exhibit strange traits. Among others, Gorges Edmund Howard mentions a characteristic anecdote of the mode of carrying the law into effect in the year 1757. After the institution of the wide-street commissioners, who were then first appointed for the purpose of opening a passage " from Essex-bridge to the royal palace, the castle of Dublin," they proceeded to carry the work into execution; but when the bargains for the houses they had purchased were concluded, the inhabitants refused to give up possession, alleging they had six months to remain; and prepared bills for

proportion to the breadth of the street, that the inhabitants were afraid the foundation part of their houses would give way and fall into it.

injunctions against the commissioners.   A host of labourers
were engaged with ladders and tools in the night before the
day on which the injunctions were to be applied for, who proceeded at the first light in the morning to strip the roofs, and
in a short time left the houses open to the sky,   The terrified
inhabitants bolted from their beds into the streets, under the
impression that the city was attacked, of which there were some
rumours, as it was a time of war.   On learning the cause they
changed their bills of injunction into bills of indictment, but
the commissioners proceeded without further impediment.

Another fatal enemy to the craft of shoeblacks was the
increase and cheapness of public vehicles.   About fifty years
after the introduction of coaches into England, the first hackney-
coach stand was established in London.   It was formed A.D.
1634, by an experimenting sea captain, named Bailey, at the
May-pole, in the Strand ; but the general use of one-horse
vehicles is of very recent introduction there, dating no farther
back than 1820, when the Londoners borrowed their cabs from
their Parisian neighbours.   The precise date of the introduction
of hackney-coaches into Dublin we know not; but the first
arrangement for regulating and controlling them was made in
1703, when their number was limited to one hundred and fifty,
and each horse employed in drawing them was required to be
" in size fourteen hands and a half, according to the standard."
The hackney-coaches we borrowed from our English neighbours, as their name imports; but our one-horse vehicles have
always been peculiar to ourselves, and were in use long before
anything of a similar kind was introduced into England.   The
earliest and rudest of these were the " Ringsend cars," so called
from their plying principally to that place and Irishtown, then
the resort of the *beau monde* for the benefit of sea-bathing.
This car consisted of a seat suspended on a strap of leather,
between shafts, and without springs.   The noise made by the
creaking of the strap, which supported the whole weight of the
company, particularly distinguished this mode of conveyance.
Its merits may be judged of by the mode in which it is alluded
to by Theophilus Cibber, in his familiar epistle to Mr. Warbur-
ton in 1753 :—" There straddles he over the buttocks of the

horse with his pedestals on the shafts, like the driver of a Ringsend car furiously driving through thick and thin, bedaubed, besplashed, besmattered, and besmeared."

The Ringsend car was succeeded by the "noddy," so called from its oscillating motion backwards and forwards. It was a low vehicle, capable of holding two persons, and drawn by one horse. It was covered with a calash, open before, but the aperture was usually filled by the "noddy-boy," who was generally a large-sized man, and occupied a seat that protruded back, so that he sat in the lap of his company. The use of the noddy by certain classes grew into a proverb—" Elegance and ease, like a shoeblack in a noddy."

The next improvement was the "jingle," a machine rolling on four wheels, but so put together that the rattling of the work was heard like the bells of a waggon team. This was finally succeeded by the jaunting-car, which still holds its place, and was, *Hibernice*, termed a *"vis-a-vis,"* because the company sit back to back. The addition of covers to the kind of cars called inside-cars, is an improvement made within the last few years, giving the vehicle most of the advantages of a coach ; since which our national vehicle has completely beaten the English importation out of the field. There is not now a single coach plying for hire on a stand in Dublin. The licensed cars amount to about 1500, being nearly equal to the number of licensed cabs in London—a fact to be accounted for probably by the absence of omnibuses here. Hackney-coaches still exist in London, but are rapidly giving place to their more youthful and active French rivals.

The jingle and jaunting-car were both in use for some time after the Union, when most of the Irish nobility became absentees, and gave occasion to the *bon mot* of the witty Duchess of Gordon, that there were but two titled men who frequented her soirees at the castle—Sir John Jingle and Sir John Jaunting-Car ; alluding to Sir John Stevenson, the celebrated musician, and Sir John Carr of pocket-book celebrity.

Before the use of one-horse cars became so general and popular, the common vehicle for a single passenger was a sedan. The introduction of sedans into England is due to King

Charles I., when a prince, and the Duke of Buckingham, who brought them from Spain.

Though the notion of " degrading Englishmen into beasts of burden" was at first exceedingly unpopular, the people soon became accustomed to it. In process of time the chair became of almost universal use. In Hogarth's time it was a very general favourite in London, especially among the fashionable. It could not exist, however, in the present crowded state of the giant metropolis, among the thunder of omnibuses and the clash of cabs; and such a thing as a sedan chair plying for hire has for some time been unknown there. Chairs still survive in our more peaceful city, but are devoted almost solely to the service of old ladies and invalids. The notion of a healthy man traversing our clean and even streets in a sedan, appears nearly as ludicrous as a man in a bonnet and petticoats; and even the fair sex of the present day seem to have resigned these solitary vehicles to the surviving members of the last generation. Far otherwise was it sixty years ago. A chair was then as indispensable to every family of distinction as a coach; and public chairs for hire were more numerous than any other public vehicle. Women always used them in cases where they would now walk; and men in full dress, in the gaudy fashion of that day, were equally unscrupulous as to the charge of effeminacy. In 1771 the number of " hackney-coaches, landaus, chariots, postchaises, and Berlins," licensed by the governors of the Foundling Hospital (in whom the jurisdiction was then vested) to ply in Dublin and the environs, was limited to three hundred, while the number of sedans was four hundred. The author of the *Philosophical Survey*, writing in 1775, says —" It is deemed a reproach for a gentlewoman to be seen walking in the streets. I was advised by my bankers to lodge in Capel Street, near Essex bridge, being in less danger of being robbed, *two chairmen* not being deemed sufficient protection." *

The Irish seem to have preferred walking with a chair to making more speed with any other conveyance. The number of Irish chairmen in London was often remarked. They made

* Phil. Survey. p. 46.

a fearful engine of attack in riots, by sawing the poles of their chairs in two, at the thick part in the middle—each pole thus supplying two terrific bludgeons.

The dangers of the streets, alluded to by the writer above quoted, were a fertile subject of complaint in the sister country, as well as here ; but the footpads of Dublin robbed in a manner, we believe, pecular to themselves. The streets were miserably lighted—indeed, in many places hardly lighted at all. So late as 1812 there were only twenty-six small oil lamps to light the immense square of Stephen's Green, which were therefore one hundred and seventy feet from one another. The footpads congregated in a dark entry, on the shady side of the street, if the moon shone; if not, the dim and dismal light of the lamps was little obstruction. A cord was provided with a loop at the end of it, The loop was laid on the pavement, and the thieves watched the approach of a passenger. If he put his foot in the loop it was immediately chucked. The man fell prostrate, and was dragged rapidly up the entry to some cellar or waste yard, where he was robbed, and sometimes murdered. The stun received by the fall usually prevented the victim from ever recognising the robbers. We knew a gentlemen who had been thus robbed, and when he recovered found himself in an alley at the end of a lane off Bride Street, nearly naked, and severely contused and lacerated by being dragged over the rough pavement.

According to Mr. Knight's account, the last London shoeblack might have been seen in 1820, in a court at the north of Fleet-street. We believe the last " regular shoeblack " in Dublin had his stand at the corner of Essex-street and Crampton-court, and disappeared at a much earlier period—more than thirty years ago. The original crafts-men, such as we have described them, were for a short time succeeded by peripatetic practitioners, who used the modern blacking that requires friction. The use of the new material, however, required too much delay and trouble, and the improvemeut never throve.

CHAPTER VIII.

SLANG SONGS — PRISON USAGES — THE NIGHT BEFORE LARRY
WAS STRETCHED — KILMAINHAM MINIT — EXECUTIONERS—
BULL BAITING—LORD ALTHAM'S BULL—THE BUSH.

AMONG the popular favourites of the last century, now almost
entirely exploded, were slang songs. As compositions their
merits were of various degrees; but the taste of the times has
so entirely changed, that their literary pretensions would now
gain them little attention. Their value chiefly consists in
being genuine pictures of uncouth scenes, not to be met with
elsewhere.

The favourite subjects of these compositions were life in a
goal and the proceedings of an execution. The interior and
discipline of a prison of this date presented a frightful contrast to the same things at the present day. The office of a
gaoler was regarded as a place of profit, of which a trade might
as fairly be driven as in the keeping of an inn; and so as the
prisoners were kept safe, and the gaoler's fees paid, the entire
object of such institutions was supposed to be answered, with
a total disregard to the improvement or correction of the unfortunate inmates. One striking instance of this is the custom
introduced in the time of King Henry the Eighth, and which
continued to a comparatively recent date, of licensing poor
prisoners to beg for their fees. When an unfortunate captive
was discharged, for want of prosecution or on acquital, the
gaoler nevertheless would not let him out, till his fees were
paid; and if he was unable to pay them from his own means,
he was allowed a certain time to beg in the neighbourhood of
the gaol, to procure them.

But the most shocking example of the utter laxity of all
discipline, and want of decency, was exhibited in the manner
in which condemned capital convicts were allowed to pass
their last hours. When so many petty offences were punishable with death, and commitment on suspicion was so often
but the stepping-stone to the gallows, it was natural that, to

the unfortunate felons themselves, an execution should be stripped of all the salutary terrors, in which alone the utility of
capital punishment consists, and should be by them regarded as
an ordinary misfortune in their course of life. The numerous
instances recorded of utter levity and recklessness, exhibited
by convicts on the very verge of eternity, clearly show this to
have been so, not merely in Ireland, but in the sister kingdom.
The practice of prisoners selling their bodies to surgeons, to be
dissected after their execution, was common, we believe, to
both countries, and the anecdote of the felon who took the
money, and then told the surgeon, laughing, that "it was a
bite, for he was to be hung in chains," we believe we can
hardly claim as Irish wit. But there was one trait, evincing
a similar careless indifference, which was peculiarly Irish. The
coffins of condemned malefactors were usually sent to them,
that the sight might suggest the immediate prospect of death,
and excite corresponding feelings of solemn reflection and pre-
paration for the awful event. From motives of humanity, the
friends of the condemned were also allowed free intercourse
with him during the brief space preceding his execution. The
result was, that the coffin was converted to a use widely different from that intended. It was employed as a card-table, and
the condemned wretch spent his last night in this world gambling on it.

A man named Lambert was an outcast of a respectable
family, and was known thus to have spent his last precious
moments; and it was on him the celebrated song of "De nite
afore Larry was stretched" is supposed to have been written.
He was a cripple, paralytic on one side, but of irreclaimable
habits. He was at once ferocious and cowardly, and was
reported to have always counselled murdering those whom he
had robbed. When on his way to execution, he shrieked and
clung with his hands to whatever was near him, and was dragged with revolting violence, by the cord about his neck, to the
gallows from which he fell; and while passing into eternity,
he vomited up the effects of his intemperate excess a few hours
before.

The celebrated song composed on him has acquired a last-

ing fame, not only as a picture of manners, but of phraseology
now passed away; and its authorship is a subject of as much
controversy as the letters of Junius. Report has conferred the
reputation of it on Burrowes, Curran, Lysaght, and others,
who have never asserted their claims. We shall mention one
more claimant, whose pretensions are equal to those of any
other. There was at that time, a man named Maher, in Waterford, who kept a cloth shop at the market cross; he had a
distorted ancle, and was known by the soubriquet of " Hurlfoot Bill." He was " a fellow of infinite humour," and his
compositions on various local and temporary subjects were in
the mouths of all his acquaintance.* There was then a literary
society established in Waterford, which received contributions
in a letter-box, that was periodically opened, and prizes awarded
for the compositions. In this was found the *first* copy of this
celebrated slang song that had been seen in Waterford. Its
merit was immediately acknowledged; inquiry was made for
its author, and " Hurlfoot Bill" presented himself, and claimed
the prize awarded. We give this anecdote, which must go
for *tantum quantum valet;* but we have heard from old members of this society, that no doubt, at the time, existed *among
them* that he was the author. His known celebrity in that
line of composition rendered it probable, and he continued to
the end of his short and eccentric career of life to claim the
authorship with confidence, " no man forbidding him."

Though "De nite afore Larry was stretched" has survived
almost all its rivals, many songs of the same style once enjoyed
nearly an equal popularity. One very similar was " Luke
Caffrey's Kilmainham Minit." The subject is also an execution, but turns on a different topic—the hope of being brought
to life by a surgical process. This hope was often the last
clung to by the dying wretch, and had some foundation in
reality, as several well-known instances are recorded in which

* There stood formerly a statue of Strongbow, in front of Reginald's Tower,
on the quay of Waterford. One Sunday morning this statue was seen converted
into that of a woman, with an inscription, supposed to be Maher's composition,
detailing circumstances which proved that it was not a statue of Strongbow, but
of Eva his wife. The metamorphosis was, however, so offensive, that this ancient
figure was removed from the conspicuous place it occupied.

it was actually effected. The unfortunate Lanigan, who was hanged at that time in Dublin, for the supposed participation in the murder of O'Flaherty, was known to be alive, and seen by many, after his public execution. When given for dissection, the use of the knife on his body had caused a flow of blood, which, in a little time, restored suspended animation. A general belief therefore existed, that opening a vein after hanging was a certain means of restoring to life—an idea particularly cherished by felons, who seldom failed to try the experiment on their departed friends. We annex specimens of this song, which, though once very popular, is now rarely met with, and, we believe, out of print.

"LUKE CAFFREY'S KILMAINHAM MINIT.

" When to see Luke's last jig we agreed,
    We tipped him our gripes in a tangle,*
Den mounted our trotters † wid speed,
    To squint at de snub as he'd dangle ;
For Luke he was ever de chap,‡
    To boozle de bull-dogs § and pinners,
And when dat he milled a fat slap,‖
    He merrily melted de winners,¶
        To snack wid de boys of de pad.**

" Along de sweet Combe den we go,
    Slap dash †† tro de Poddle we lark it,
But when dat we come to de Row,‡‡
    Oh, dere was no meat §§ in de market ;

We subjoin a glossary of some of the unintelligible phrases.

* " Tipped our gripes in a tangle." A strong figurative expression for an earnest shake of many hands.

† " Mounted our trotters," synonymous with " riding shank's mare."

‡ " Chap," a contraction of chapman, a dealer in small wares—similar to the epithet of " small merchant," applied to a boy.

§ " Boozle de bull-dogs," &c., outwit thief-takers and gaolers.

‖ " Milled a fat slap," made a rich booty.

¶ " Melted the winners," spent the booty—winners, by mytonymy for winnings.

** " Boys of the Pad," footpads, robbers. Paddington, a village near London, once infamous for such, means " the town of robbers."

†† " Slap dash," &c. The Poddle was a low street over the stream of that name, always flooded and dirty ; the passengers waded through it like " mud larks."

‡‡ " Come to de Row," New-row, where the prison was then.

§§ " Meat," a human body : " seeing the cold meat home," was attending a funeral.

De boy he had travelled afore,*
  Like rattlers, we after him pegged it;
To miss him, would grieve us full sore,
  Case why, as a favour he begged it—
    We'd tip him the fives † fore his det."

They come up with him before he is turned off, and the
following dialogue ensues:—

    " ' Your sowl, I'd fight blood to de eyes,
      You know it, I would to content ye,
    But foul play I always despise—
      Dat's for one for to fall upon twenty.'
    Ses he, ''Tis my fate for to die,
      I knowd it when I was committed,
    But if dat de slang you run sly,
      De scrag-boy ‡ may yet be outwitted,
      And I scout again on de lay.

    " ' When I dance twixt de ert and de skyes,
      De clargy may bleet for de struggler,
    Bud when on de ground your friend lies,
      Oh, tip me a snig in de jugglar;
    Ye know dat is all my last hope,
      As de surgents of ottamy § tell us,
    Dat when I'm cut down from de rope,
      You'd bring back de puff to my bellows,
      And set me once more on my pins.'

    " Dese last words were spoke wid a sigh.
      We saw de poor fellow was funkin,
    De drizzle stole down from his eye,
      Do we tought he had got better spunk in;
    Wid a tip of de slang we replied,
      And a blinker dat nobody noted,
    De clargy stept down from his side,
      And de dust-cart ‖ from under him floated,
      And left him to dance on de air.

    " Pads foremost he dived, and den round,¶.
      He capered de Kilmainham minit,

* "Travelled afore," set out for Stephen's-green, where the gallows then was.
† " Tip me de fives," five fingers—shake hands.
‡ "Scrag-boy," hangman—from scrag, the neck.
§ " Ottamy," anatomy.
‖ " Dust-cart," the flat platform cart provided for the accommodation of the
doomed, before the invention of prison drops.
¶ "Pads foremost he dived, and den round." This is horribly graphic, as those
who have unfortunately chanced to witness such a scene can testify.

> But when dat he lay on de ground,
>> Our bisness we tought to begin it;
> Wid de stuff to a shebeen* we hied,
>> But det had shut fast every grinder,
> His brain-box hung all a one side,
>> And no distiller's pig could be blinder;
>>> But dat's what we all must come to.

> "His disconsolate widdy† came in
>> From tipping the scrag-boy a dustin—"

The poet then records her melancholy situation, in the prospect of being soon a mother, and concludes thus:—

> "We tipped him a snig as he said,
>> In de juggler, oh dere where de mark is,
> Bud when dat we found him quite ded,
>> In de dust-case we bundled his carcase,
>>> For a Protestant lease of the sod."‡

We may mention in passing, that one circumstance which contributed to the strange contradiction exhibited at an Irish execution, turning that awful scene into an opportunity for merriment and jest, was the character and dress of the hangman. That functionary was generally disguised in a fantastic manner, very ill suited to the occasion. On his face he wore a grotesque mask, and on his back an enormous hump, in the whole resembling Punch in the puppet show. The original design of this apparent levity was, to protect the executioner by the disguise; and it was in some degree necessary. The use he made of the hump was curious. It was formed of a large wooden bowl-dish, laid between his shoulders, and covered with his clothes. When the criminal was turned off, and the

---

* "Shebeen," a low public-house, where a weak small-beer was sold for a farthing a quart. It was in high request, as connected with the family of St. Patrick, for we are told in the song—
> "His mother kept a shebeen shoe
> In the town of Enniskillen."

† "His disconsolate widdy." It is a remarkable fact that felons were generally attended by females in the family way, who had various duties to perform: the first was to *dust*, *i. e.*, abuse the hangman; the second to beg for the funeral. See p. 91.

‡ "Protestant lease of the sod." In allusion to the penal laws, which prohibited Roman Catholics from acquiring long titles.

"dusting of the scrag-boy" began, the hangman was assailed, not merely with shouts and curses, but often with showers of stones. To escape the latter, he ducked down his head, and opposed his hump as a shield, from which the missiles rebounded with a force that showed how soon his skull would have been fractured if exposed to them. After some antics, the finisher of the law dived among the sheriff's attendants, and disappeared. This grotesque figure, surrounded by two or more human beings, struggling in the awful agonies of a violent and horrible death, was regarded by the mob as presenting a funny and jocular contrast.

Many anecdotes are recorded of the levity of hangmen eminent in their day. The last and most notorious of the craft was "Tom Galvin." He is not very long dead, and in his old age was often visited at Kilmainham gaol by persons who indulged a morbid curiosity to see him and the rope with which he had hanged most of his own nearest relations. One of his practical facetiæ was, to slip the rope slily round a visitor's neck and give it a sudden chuck, which would nearly cause the sensation of strangling. He was brutally unfeeling in the discharge of his horrid duty, and when a reprieve would come to some wretch whose hanging he anticipated, he would almost cry with disappointment at the loss of his fee, and say, "it is a hard thing to be taking the bread out of the mouth of an old man like me!" He was always impatient at any delay made by a convict. When the wretched Jemmy O'Brien was about to be executed, he exhibited the greatest terror, and lingered over his devotions, to protract his life thus for a few moments. Galvin's address to him is well known. He called out at the door, so as to be heard by all the bystanders, as well as the criminal, " Mr. O'Brien, jewel, *long life* to you, make haste wid your prayers; de people is getting tired under de swing-swong."

The history of the last century in Ireland presents instances of unprofessional executioners, whose actions would be even more grotesque if they were not so revolting, that horror supersedes every other feeling respecting them. The best known is the case of Lieutenant Hepenstal, commemorated by

Barrington, who, however, is mistaken in his account of him. He was in the Wicklow militia, and a very tall man. On one occasion, in Westmeath, his corps being in want of a gallows to hang "a croppy," Hepenstal volunteered to execute him without one, and actually hanged the wretched man by swinging him over his own shoulder with a drum cord. He owes his name of "Walking Gallows" to the following epigram:—

> "This county owes you many thanks,
> And will reward your friendly pranks,
> But what fresh evils may befal us,
> Now that we've lost our walking gallows!"

But the brutality of Hepenstal is left in the shade by the contrast presented by a *female* hangman. In August, 1793, a gang of robbers were surrounded and captured near Bruff. One of them was a Margaret Farrell. Among her duties one was to find the cord for the execution of persons who were sacrificed to the vengeance of the gang. On an occasion, when she was at a loss for a cord, she stripped off her clothes, and taking her chemise tore it into strips, which she twisted, tied round the neck of the wretched man who was doomed to suffer, and, when he was swung up to a neighbouring tree, complacently contemplated the strength of the contrivance till he died.

Another slang song, once in great celebrity, but now nearly forgotten, is "Lord Altham's Bull." As it is little known, and, we believe, not to be obtained in print, and is, perhaps, the most graphic of its class, and the best specimen of the slang of sixty years ago, we subjoin a few extracts from it also. We should premise that the subject of the song—a bull bait— though the humanity of modern legislation has now very properly prohibited it—was, at the time of which we speak, not merely a very common and popular sport among the lower orders, but, like prize-fighting and the cock-pit, often keenly relished by the better classes of society. This was not merely owing to the grosser tastes of the age, but in a great measure to peculiar circumstances. Ireland was then a pastoral country, with little agriculture and less manufactures. It was the great grazing ground on which were fed all the cattle that supplied the armies of England, in their incessant wars then waged for the balance of power in Europe, the subjugation of revolted colonies in America, or counteracting the revolutionary principles of France. The midland counties of Ireland, particularly Tipperary, now waving with corn, were one great bullock walk; and Cork, Waterford and Dublin were the marts where the beasts were slaughtered and prepared for exportation.

Among the cattle sent in was a large proportion of bulls. The south of Ireland, connected by several ties with Spain, adopted many Spanish usages and sports; among the rest, bull-fighting, which degenerated into bull-baiting. In Waterford and other towns, on the election of every mayor, he was surrounded by a mob, who shouted out, "a rope, a rope, a rope!" and the new mayor never failed to grant their demands. A rope two inches in diameter, with a competent leather collar and buckle, had been previously prepared, and was then delivered to the claimants, who bore it away in triumph, and deposited it in the city gaol-yard, to remain there till wanted. We have an extract before us from the old corporation books of Waterford, dated 1714, October, in which month the slaughtering season commenced:—"Ordered, that a bull-rope be provided at the charge of the city revenue." Under this sanction, the populace assumed the authority of seizing all the bulls, and driving them to the bull-ring to be baited before they were killed. The place for baiting them was an open space outside the city gate, called Ballybricken. It was surrounded with houses, from which spectators looked on, as at a Spanish bull-fight. In the centre was the ring through which the rope was passed. It was surmounted by a pole, bearing a large copper bull on a vane. In 1798, when bull-baits were prohibited, this apparatus was removed, and the sport discontinued; but prior to that it was followed with the greatest enthusiasm; and it was not unusual to see eighteen or twenty of these animals baited during the season.

To enhance and render perfect this sport, a peculiar breed of dogs was cherished; the purity of whose blood is marked by small stature, with enormous, disproportioned heads and jaws, the upper short and snub, and the under projecting beyond it.

The savage ferocity and tenacity of those small animals are quite extraordinary. A single one unsupported would seize a fierce bull by the lip or nose, and pin to the ground the comparatively gigantic animal, as if he had been fixed with a stake of iron. Even after the fracture of their limbs, they never relax their hold; and it was often necessary, at the conclusion of a day's sport, to cut off broken legs, and in that mutilated state they were seen on three legs rushing at the bull.

When, on rare occasions, a rope was refused by a refractory mayor, or a new one was required, the bull was driven through the streets of the town, and sometimes even into his worship's shop or hall, as a hint of what was wanted, and the civic authorities were often called out with the military to repress the riots that ensued. Lives were frequently lost, and a Lord Mayor of Dublin was long remembered by the name of "Alderman Levellow," for his interference on such an occasion. A bull was driven through the lower part of Abbey-street, then open and called the "lots," and the mob became so riotous that the military were called out and ordered to fire. They directed their muskets above the heads of the people, but the Lord Mayor laying his rod on them, depressed them to a murderous level, and several persons were killed. This, we believe, was the last bull-bait recorded in Dublin, and the restrictive regulations adopted at the time of the rebellion in '98, prohibiting the assemblage of persons, suppressed bull-baiting then, and it was never since revived.

The custom of seizing bulls on their way to market, for the purpose of baiting, became so grievous an evil in Dublin in 1779, that it was the subject of a special enactment, making it a peculiar offence to take a bull from the drivers for such a purpose, on its way too or from market.* The place for bull-baiting in Dublin was in the Corn-market, where there was an iron ring, to which the butchers fastened the animals they baited. An officer, called the "Mayor of the bull-ring," had a singular jurisdiction allowed to him. He was the guardian of bachelors, and it was a duty of his office to take cognizance of their conduct. After the marriage ceremony, the bridal party

* Statute, 19, 20, George III., c. 36.

were commonly conducted to the ring by "the mayor" and his attendants, when a kiss from "his worship" to the bride concluded the ceremony, from which they went home with the bridegroom, who entertained them according to his ability.

Having premised so much, we give an example of

LORD ALTHAM'S BULL.*

"'Twas on the fust of sweet Magay,
    It being a high holiday,
    Six and twenty boys of de straw†
Went to take Lord Altham's bull away.

" *Spoken*—I being de fust in de field, who should I see bud de mosey wid his horns sticking in de ground. Well becomes me, I pinked up to him, ketched him by de tail, and rode him dree times round de field, as well as ever de master of de tailor's corporation rode de fringes ;‡ but de mosey being game to de back bone, de first rise he gev me in de elements, he made a smash of me collar-bone. So dere being no blunt in de cly,§ Madame Stevens was de word,‖ where I lay for seven weeks in lavendar, on de broad of me back, like Paddy Ward's pig,¶ be de hokey.**

* As the allusions and phraseology of this composition are now nearly obsolete, a few explanatory notes on the text may be necessary.

+ "Boys of de straw !"—Citizens of the straw market, Smithfield, a locality still distinguished as the residence of a bull-baiting progeny.

‡ " Fringes "—the name by which the triennial procession of the trades was known—a corruption of "franchises." The masters rode at the head of their corporations, and the tailors were never distinguished as first-rate horsemen. We have already given an account of this extraordinary ceremony. The last, we believe, took place on the election of Grattan to the representation of Dublin. Those who remember it say O'Connell's late procession of the trades was a poor imitation of it.

§ " No blunt in de cly."—No money in the pocket.

‖ "Madame Stevens was de word."—Miss Griselda Stevens was left by her brother, an eminent physician in Dublin, an estate in Westmeath and the King's County, yielding £600 per annum, for her life; and after her death to found an hospital. She, however, most benevolently commenced the application of it to the donor's charitable intentions during her life. She founded in 1720 the celebrated hospital near Kilmainham, which bears her name, and has ever since been the gratuitous receptacle of the maimed and poor, particularly for sudden accidents, as the inscription on the door declares—" Ægris sauciisque sanandis." Larry, therefore, means he had to betake himself to the hospital, where he had nothing to pay.

¶ " Paddy Ward's pig."—Who Paddy Ward was, we believe, has eluded the inquiries of historians and antiquaries. He was, however, very eminent for his sayings and doings : he measured a griddle, and declared it was "as broad as it was long !" Hence, his "griddle" was as famous an illustration as his pig.

** " Be de hokey !"—A form of adjuration condensing into one, two words, "holy poker !"—a supposed implement of purgatory held in much awe.

" We drove de bull tro many a gap,
    And kep him going many a mile,
    But when we came to Kilmainham lands,
    We let de mosey rest awhile.

" *Spoken*—Oh ! boys, if de mosey was keeper of de ancle-spring warehouse,* you cud not help pitying him ; his hide smoked like Ned Costigan's brewery,† and dere was no more hair on his hoofs dan dere's wool on a goose's gams,‡ be de hokey.

" We drove de bull down sweet Truck-street,
    Widout eider dread or figear,
    When out run Mosey Creathorn's§ bitch,
    Hand cotched de bull be de year.

" *Spoken*—Hye, Jock—dat dog's my bitch‖—spit on her nose to keep her in wind—fight fair, boys, and no stones—low, Nettle, low¶—shift, shift, my beauty, and keep your hoult. Oh ! boys, your souls, I tought de life ud leave Mosey Creathorn's glimms, when he saw his bitch in de air ; ' Oh ! Larry Casey, happy det to you, and glory may you get, stand wide and ketch her in your arms—if her head smacks de pavement, she's not worth lifting up—dat's right, yer sowls, now tip her a sup a de blood while it's warm.'

" We drove de bull down Corn-market,
    As all de world might segee,
    When brave Tedy Foy trust his nose tro' de bars,
    Crying ' High for de sweet liberty.'**

* " Ancle-spring warehouse," an ingenious periphrasis for the stocks.

† " Ned Costigan,"—a celebrated Dublin distiller, whose premises were long famous for adumbrating the liberties with their smoke.

‡ " Gams !"—Legs : from the French *Jambes*. Nothing, perhaps, could more forcibly describe the total absence of hair from the poor bull's legs than the state of a goose's gam.

§ " Creathorn."—A respectable name long appearing among the commons and freemen of the butchers' guild.

‖ " Dat dog's my bitch !"—This confusion of genders is not confined to Mosey Creathorn. His late Majesty, George IV., when Prince of Wales, was notoriously fond of bull-baiting. On one occasion, a Smithfield butcher slapped him on the back in ecstacy, crying out, with an imprecation, "d—— your blood, Mr. Prince, the dog that pinned the bull is my bitch !"

¶ " Low, Nettle !—low !—and keep your hoult !"—Taking a bull by the ear, was the mark of a mongrel. The perfection of a bull-dog was, to seize the bull by the nose, and hold fast—so Nettle is ordered to shift, but keep her hold, *i. e.*, move down to the nose without letting go. Limbs were often broken by the tossing of the bull, and amputated, which, however, did not repress the animal's ardour ; and many a " three-legged bitch " acquired great celebrity, after losing her limb.

** " Corn-market."—The old prison stood in this street, and was called " Newgate," because it had been once a gate of the city. In 1773 the new prison was built, and the old taken down. Corn-market lay in the way from Kilmainham

"*Spoken*—Oh! cruel Coffey, glory to you, just knock off my darbies—let me out on padroul of honour*—I'll expel de mob—kill five, skin six, and be de fader of de scity, I'll return like an innocent lamb to de sheep-walk. 'Oh! boys, who lost an arm,† who lost five fingers and a tumb?' 'Oh!' says Larry Casey, 'it belongs to Luke Ochy, I know it by de slime on de slieve.'

> "De mosey took down Plunket-street,‡
> Where de clothes on de pegs were hanging,
> Oh! den he laid about wid his nob,
> De shifts around him banging.

"*Spoken*—Oh! Mrs. Mulligan, jewel, take in de bits o' duds from de wall, out o' de way o' de mosey's horns—be de hokey, he'll fly kites wid dem, and den poor Miss Judy will go de Lady Mayress's ball, like a spatchcock.

> "Lord Altham is a very bad man,
> As all de neighbours know,
> For driving white Roger from Kilmainham lands,
> We all to Virginy must go!

"*Spoken*—Well! boys!—suppose we go for seven years, an't dere six of us! Dat's just fourteen monts a-piece.§ I can sail in a turf-kish, and if ever I come back from his Majesty's tobacco-manufactory,‖ I'll butter my knife in his tripes, and give him his guts for garters. All de world knows I've de blood of de Dempseys in me."

to the city market, near Plunket-street, which, therefore, the bull had to pass through; and this causes Teddy Foy's affecting aspiration after liberty, with his nose through the bars.

* "Padroul"—Parole of honour.

† "Who lost an arm," &c.—Larey Casey's mark of recognition of the owner is not merely graphic, but, coarse as it may appear, is very classical. The father of Horace, it seems, was addicted to Luke Ochy's habits, which caused his adversaries to say—"Quoties vidi cubito se emungentem."—See præfat. Hor. Sat. Ed. Delph.

‡ "Plunket-street," long distinguished as the mart in Dublin for the sale of old clothes, whence the proverb, to describe a person dressed in second-hand finery, that he "stripped a peg in Plunket-street." It is in the immediate vicinity of the scene of action.

§ "Dat's but fourteen monts a-piece!"—Larry Dempsey's calculation may appear not according to the rules of arithmetic, however it may be to those of sentiment. Miss Edgeworth we believe it is who remarks, that such Irishisms are founded on sociability of temper. The two Irishmen transported for fourteen years, who comforted themselves, because it was but seven years a-piece, were consoled with the reflection, that the enjoyment of each other's society would make the time appear to each but half its real length.

‖ "His Majesty's Tobacco Manufactory."—This may seem merely a metaphor of Larry's; but is nevertheless legally correct, and borrowed from parliamentary phraseology. The language of all statutes previous to the 30 George III. was, "transportation to His Majesty's plantations in North America."

We shall conclude with specimens from one more song, very popular in its day. We have before noticed the feuds between the Liberty and Ormond boys. Various objects of petty display presented objects of emulation and strife. Among them was planting a May-bush—one party endeavouring to cut down what the other had set up. A memorable contest of this kind in which the weavers cut down " the bush" of the butchers, is thus celebrated in song :—

" DE MAY-BUSH.

" De night afore de fust of Magay
      Ri rigidi, ri ri dum dee,
   We all did agree without any delay,
   To cut a May-bush, so we pegged it away,
      Ri rigidi dum dee !"

The leader of the boys was Bill Durham, a familiar corruption of Dermot, his right name, a distinguished man at that time in the Liberty riots. When the tree was cut down, it was borne back in triumph, with Bill astride on it, exhibiting a classical picture still more graphic than the gem of Bacchus astride on his tun :—

" Bill Durham, he sat astride on his bush,
      Ri rigidi, ri ri dum dee,
   And dere he kept singin', as sweet as a trush—
   His faulchin in one hand, his pipe in his mush—*
      Ri rigidi dum dee !"

" The Bush" having been planted in Smithfield, contributions were raised to do it honour ; and among other contributors were the fishwomen of Pill-lane, who, from contiguity of situation and similarity of dealing, were closely allied to the butchers of Ormond market. A custom prevailed here, of selling the fish brought for sale, to the women who retailed it, by auction. The auctioneer, who was generally one of themselves, holding a plaice or a haddock by the tail, instead of a hammer, knocked down the lot to the highest bidder. This was an important time to the trade ; yet the high-minded poissardes, like their Parisian sisters, " sacrificed every thing to their patriotic feel-

* " In his mush "—mouth, from the French *mouche*. Many words are similarly derived—gossoon, a boy, from *garcon*, &c.

ings," and abandoned the market, *even* at this crisis, to attend
" de bush :"—

> " From de lane* came each lass in her holiday gown,
>   Ri rigidi ri ri dum dee,
> Do de haddock was up, and de lot was knocked down,
> Dey doused all dere sieves,† till dey riz de half-crown,‡
>   Ri rigidi dum dee !"

After indulging in the festivities of the occasion round " de
bush," some returned, and some lay about *vino somnoque
sepulti ;* and so, not watching with due vigilance, the Liberty
boys stole on their security, cut down, and carried of " de bush."
The effect on Bill Durham when he heard the adversary passing on their way back with the trophy, is thus described :—

> " Bill Durham, being up de nite afore,
>   Ri rigidi ri ri dum dee,
> Was now in his flea-park,§ taking a snore,
> When he heard de mob pass by his door,
>   Ri rigidi dum dee !

> " Den over his shoulders his flesh-bag he trew,
>   Ri rigidi ri ri dum dee,
> And out of the chimbley his faulchion he drew,
> And, mad as a hatter, down May-lane he flew,
>   Ri rigidi dum dee !

> " Wid his hat in his hand by de way of a shield,
>   Ri rigidi ri ri dum dee,
> He kep all along crying out ' never yield !'
> But he never cried stop till he came to Smithfield
>   Ri rigidi dum dee !

---

* "De lane."—Pill-lane, called so, *par excellence*, as the great centre and
mart of piscatory dealing.

† "Doused all dere sieves."—Laid them down at their uncle's, the pawn-
broker's.

‡ "Riz half-a-crown."—The neuter verb, "rise," is classically used here for
the active verb, "raised," a common licence with our poets.

§ "Flea-park."—This appellation of Bill's bed was no doubt borrowed from
the account the Emperor Julian gives of his beard, "I permit little beasts,"
said he, "to run about it, like animals in a park." The word he uses is φθειεις
pediculi; so that Durham's "flea-park" was evidently sanctioned by the
Emperor's "—park." The Abbe de Bletterie, who translated Julian's work,
complains that he was accused for not suppressing the image presented by
Julian ; but adds very properly, *la delicatesse Francaise va-t-elle jus'qu au fal-
sifier les auteurs ?* So we say of our author.

" Dere finding no bush, but de watch-boys all flown,
　　　Ri rigidi ri ri dum dee,
　Your sowls, says Bill Durham, I'm left all alone
　Be de hokey, de glory of Smidfield is gone !—
　　　Ri rigidi dum dee !''

Bill vows revenge in a very characteristic and professional manner, by driving one of the bulls of Ormond-market among his adversaries :—

" For de loss of our bush, revenge we will get,
　　　Ri rigidi ri ri dum dee,
　In de slaughtering season we'll tip 'em a sweat,
　　　Rigidi di do dee,
　We'll wallop a mosey down Mead-street in tune,
　And we won't leave a weaver alive on de Coombe ;
　But we'll rip up his tripe-bag, and burn his loom.
　　　Ri rigidi di do dee !''

CHAPTER IX.

RAPPAREES AND ROBBERS—HEDGE SCHOOLS—FRENEY—NOR-
THERN ROBBERS—SHAWN CROSSACH—WILLIAM CROTTY—
CROTTY'S LAMENT—FELON'S BODIES—FREDERICK CAUL-
FIELD.

IF the moral conduct of a people is formed by the instruction of their early years, it is not difficult to account for the great laxity observed in the conduct of the lower orders in Ireland half a century ago. It is true the excellent schools of the Incorporated Society, inculcating religion, morality, and obedience to the laws, in the different counties, were like beacons spreading light around·them to a certain extent ; but they were comparatively few and far between, and the unceasing objects of calumny and attack ; and, in fact, the only places of general instruction were " Hedge Schools," that is, benches laid loosely either in a waste cabin, or under a hedge by the way-side, where the only books of instruction were sixpenny volumes, named " Burton Books." They were small octavos, bound in cheap white basil, the paper and type of the coarsest kind, and full of typographical errors, illustrated occasionally by plates of the most "uncouth sculpture." But the rudeness of the book was a trifling defect compared with its contents. The general character of such volumes was loose and immoral, Among them, two were most popular—"Laugh and be fat," and "The Irish Rogues and Rapparees." The first was a collection of the most indecent stories, told in the coarsest language; the second celebrated the deeds of highwaymen. By the one, the moral sense of the children of both sexes was corrupted, by teaching them to indulge in what was gross and indelicate; by the other, their integrity and sense of right and wrong was confounded, by proposing the actions of lawless felons as objects of interest and imitation. Among the rapparees was one held in high esteem by the youth of the peasantry, and a representation of his deeds formed a part of their plays and sports. This person was James Freney.

He was born in the house of Mr. Robbins, a respectable gentleman, in the county of Kilkenny, where his father was a servant. He showed an early dislike to every thing that was praiseworthy and of "good report," and no efforts of his kind patron could turn him from low dissipation. He had a precocious and incorrigible fondness for cock-fighting, hurling, and gambling. His friends at length were compelled to abandon him to his own irregular courses, and he became a highwayman. He collected round him all the idle and worthless fellows of the neighbourhood, whom he formed into a gang of robbers, and over whom he exercised absolute control, an object of alarm and terror to Kilkenny and the neighbouring counties. The manner of their proceeding was very summary. When a house was *set* to be robbed, he proceeded to a forge in the vicinity, and ordering one of his gang to open it and take out a sledge, they went at once to the house, dashed in the door or windows, and rifled it of all its valuable property. Such was the terror they excited, and the system of violence they pursued, that they were rarely opposed. During the day they stopped travellers, and robbed on the highway, and even levied black mail on carmen, openly demanding a ransom for the goods they seized. The usual conveyance for shop goods from large to small towns, were common cars; spies were set, and the approach of the cars with goods announced to Freney, who met them at a convenient place, drove them to a thicket, or some near mountain, set a ransom on their value, and then dismissed one of their drivers to report the loss, and bring back the ransom, which was rarely withheld. On one occasion, five cars proceeding from Waterford to Thomastown, loaded with valuable shop goods, were thus stopped, their ransom set down at £150, and one of the drivers sent to fetch it. While Freney was, as usual, waiting for the return, in confident expectation, one of his scouts ran back with information that a body of the merchants of Waterford, accompanied by a strong force of the militia, were near at hand to take him. He looked out, and saw the road beset on all sides. He ran, and after some pursuit, concealed himself in a cleft of a rock covered by furze and brambles. Here he laid his loaded musket across his body, and a case of cocked pistols at each side of him, and after waiting for some time, expecting his pursuers, he fell fast asleep. One of the party in search of him heard him snoring, looked in, and having ascertained who it was, immediately ran to announce to the pursuers his discovery. Freney was immediately surrounded by the *posse*, who began firing into the spot where he lay. The sound awakened him, and he saw the ground about him riddled and torn by the balls, which passed over his body. He lay still until some of the party, supposing he must be dead, were about to pull him out by the legs, when he suddenly started up, and rushed out with his musket cocked. The terror of his name, and the suddenness of his appearance, frightened the party, They all, military and mercantile, ran off in different directions, each man alarmed for his own safety; while Freney, availing himself of the momentary panic, escaped under cover of a neighbouring hedge. He met a spancelled horse, and cutting the cords with his knife, mounted on its back, and rode off, under a shower of balls, to the river Nore, not far distant; this he dashed into, swam across, and found himself in safety at the other side, his pursuers stopping on the bank of the river, and firing at him without effect, as he crossed the opposite fields.

By such daring deeds and hair-breadth escapes as these he astonished the country, and kept it in alarm, and, to a certain degree, in subjection, for five years. No one thought of resisting him on the highway, or defending a house when attacked, or refusing the ransom for goods when demanded. But at length his gang, one by one, melted away. They turned informers against each other, and were hanged in succession, till but one, named Bulger, remained with him. They were " set " in a cabin, and in making their escape, Bulger was wounded by a ball in his leg, but his companion took him on his back, and they both escaped. Freney now seeing no prospect of safety to himself, determined to purchase it by the sacrifice of his last friend. He had him set, and delivered into the hands of justice, and thus saw the last of his gang convicted and executed. For his treachery on this occasion, his own pardon was secured by the interest of Lord Carrick, and a small situation in the revenue was given to him in the town of New Ross, in which he continued many years. Several gentlemen visited him, to hear him tell his adventures, which he freely communicated. He ultimately wrote his autobiography, which became one of the most popular school-books in our *system* of education sixty years ago. His adventures were the favourite themes of school-boys, and the representation of his achievements their favourite amusement. His robbery on the highway, his bursting open houses, his exacting ransom were faithfully enacted, particularly the scene of his escape from the Waterford militia, and his carrying off his companion, Bulger, with a wounded leg. In effect, the consequence said to have followed from Schiller's Robbers on the youth of Germany, was realised among the young peasantry of Ireland.

Freney is still well remembered in the south-east of Ireland. On the road between Clonmel and Kilkenny, the scene of many of his robberies, an elm is pointed out to the traveller, which is known as " Freney's tree." His character has been much overrated, as represented by some novel writers. He had nothing of dignified appearance or gentlemanly manners. Those who saw and conversed with him described him as a mean-looking fellow, pitted with the small-pox, and blind of an eye, whence

Freney became a *soubriquet* for all persons who had lost an eye. He was not of a sanguinary disposition, and was susceptible of grateful attachment. His most determined pursuer was a Mr. Robbins, who often nearly captured him, but he never could be prevailed on to take his life, though it was often in his power, because he was one of the family to whose kindness he was early indebted. He had no such feeling, however, for his companion, Bulger, who often saved his life. He betrayed him, like others of his gang, to insure his own pardon. He was a coarse, vulgar, treacherous villain, much of the highwayman, and nothing of the hero.

While Freney gained fame in the south, many of his fraternity, Redmond O'Hanlon and others, are commemorated in the same books as achieving renown in the north. Indeed, the last of the highwaymen was a northern, named Collyer, who infested the roads to Drogheda so lately as within the last thirty years. One of the northern rapparees is distinguished for a singular trait of character. "Shawn Crossach" was an old freebooter, who infested the counties of Derry and Tyrone. He had two sons, whom he educated from their earliest days in acts of robbery. He placed a pot of stirabout in the centre of his cabin, between two doors, and no boy got his supper who was not able to take it by force or fraud from his father. One of them, "Paurya Fhad," or "Young Paddy," was a distinguished proficient in free-booting. Their robbery of an officer of rank, of a considerable treasure, is yet commemorated by the name of the bridge where it was effected, which is called "the General's Bridge." For this daring deed on a high functionary, they were all apprehended, tried, and convicted. After sentence was passed, it was represented that two victims would be a sufficient example to satisfy justice, and mercy might be shown to the old man. They were all, however, led out to execution ; but at the gallows, the father was told that he was pardoned by the mercy of government. He looked no way glad, but the contrary, and at first offered to exchange the pardon with " Paurya Fhad," his youngest son. When he was informed that this could not be allowed, he said, after a short deliberation, " Well, I'm an old man, anyhow, and can't live long, and what use will pardon be to me! so, wi' the blessing o' God, I'll shake a foot wi' the boys." He persisted in his determination, and would listen to no persuasion against his right to be hanged, and have his sentence executed; so he suffered between his two sons, holding affectionately one of their hands at each side.

But more eminent than any of these we have mentioned, though prior in time, was a rapparee, named William Crotty. The habits and usages which English writers of the sixteenth century impute to the " wild Irish," were not wholly extinct eighty years ago.   Men from the woods and mountains infested the neighbourhood of populous towns, having holes and dens from which they issued to commit their depredations, and to which they retired, like wild beasts to their lair; when pursued, they thus suddenly sunk into the earth and disappeared, and were passed by their pusuers.   They lived like the subjects of the Irish chieftain, who pronounced a malediction on any of his tribe that would dwell in a house built with hands.   The den of the modern rapparee was usually in a situation commanding a view of the road, from which he could pounce, like a vulture on his quarry, on the passengers, and return with his prey to his rock.   Such was the mode of life of Crotty.   His den, still known as " Crotty's Hole," is on the south-eastern point of the Comeragh mountains, in the west of the county of Waterford.   It is on an eminence commanding a view of the subjacent country, east and west, almost from Dungarvan to Carrick, and south, to Tramore.   There is scarcely a place in Ireland commanding a more evtensive view of high roads. The eminence is accessible from below with some difficulty, and the descent into " the hole" is very steep and precipitous.

The interior of this cave consists of one large chamber, from which branch off some smaller recesses.   These were occupied by Crotty for sleeping and other domestic purposes; but tradition assigns to them a more horrible use.   Crotty was reputed to be a cannibal, and he was believed to fill these recesses with stores of human flesh, on which he fed.   Hence he was called the " Irish Sawny Bean," after the Highland robber of that name, who is said to have had a taste for the same diet.

Crotty was a man of desperate courage and unequalled personal agility; often baffling pursuers even when mounted on fleet horses. His accomplice was a man named David Norris, who was superior to Crotty in ability and the cunning of his craft, though his inferior in strength and activity. Their depredations were usually designed by Norris, and entrusted to Crotty for execution; and Norris often stimulated Crotty to acts of violence and wanton cruelty, to which he would have been otherwise indisposed. Among other instances of their barbarity recorded by tradition is the following :—Passing one night by a cabin on the road-side, they saw a light in the window; on looking in, they perceived a man and his wife at their supper; the former of whom having peeled a potato, was raising it to his mouth. " Now, for any bet," said Crotty, " the ball in my pistol shall pass his lips before the potato." He fired, and the poor man fell dead, the ball having pierced his mouth while yet the potato was at his lips. Crotty was afterwards taken, having been disabled by a shot in the mouth, and the peasantry, to this day, affirm it was the judgment of heaven inflicted on him for this act of cruelty.

Though well known personally to all the county, Crotty never hesitated to appear at fairs and markets, where he was generally well received. Like many other highwaymen he was in the habit of sharing with the poor what he plundered from the rich; and thus acquired popularity sufficient to procure him immediate warning of any danger which might threaten him. He frequented the fair green of Kilmacthomas, and openly joined with the young men in hurling and foot-ball on Sunday evenings, danced with the girls at wakes and patterns, and familiarly entered respectable houses. He once visited a widow lady, named Rogers, near Tramore, while she was entertaining a large company at dinner. The guests were terror-stricken when he stalked into the room and displayed his arms; but he calmly desired a servant to give him the plate on the side-board, and his direction being instantly complied with, he walked out without committing any further depredation. The servant was immediately charged with being his accomplice, and threatened with prosecution; whereupon he ran after Crotty, and implored him to restore the plate.   Crotty complied, turned to the house, and handed back the property to Mrs. Rogers.   She was profuse in her thanks, but he desired her to observe he was only lending the plate to her, and peremtorily demanded it back.   She again surrendered it, and he said—" Now, madam, remember it was you, and not your servant, who gave this to me, and do not charge him with the loss."   Such was the terror of his name that no attempt was made to pursue him.

Crotty's depredations becoming intolerable, and his retreat known, a gentleman, named Hearn, who lived within three miles of it, at length determined to capture him.   Hearn was a man of uncommon strength and indomitable resolution.   He bribed Norris's wife to give him notice when Crotty would be found " at home."   She met Mr. Hearn one day on the road, and as she passed, said slily, and without looking at him, " the bird's in the nest."   He was unaccompanied, but, being well armed, he acted on the hint, and went directly to " the hole."   He called Crotty by his Christian name, " William," and the robber, without suspicion, came up.   The moment his head appeared, Mr. Hearn, knowing he must be well armed and his desperate character, fired at him, and wounded him severely in the mouth.   He succeeded, however, in effecting his escape. Mr. Hearn determined still to watch him ; and in a short time afterwards, received secret information from Norris's wife that Crotty was in Norris's house.   He proceeded thither directly, well armed, and took Crotty by surprise, who was wholly unprepared, and imagined himself secure.   The latter submitted to be arrested, without further resistance, saying, he long knew Mr. Hearn was the man who would take him.

As in many of his countrymen, the extremes of ferocity and kindly feeling were combined in Crotty.   When Mr. Hearn was leading him away, he asked him why, as he lived so near, and had so frequent opportunities of taking his life, he had not done so.   " I often intended it," said the malefactor ; " and last Christmas I went to shoot you; but I saw through the parlour window you and your wife and children sitting so happily round the fire, that though I had the pistol cocked and you

covered, my heart failed me, and I could not draw the trigger.
I often followed you, too, when you were fishing in the Clodagh;
but your son was with you, and I felt sure if I killed *you*, he
would shoot *me*, and I could not bring myself to take both your
lives."

The gun with which Crotty was shot is preserved and
shown as a curiosity at Shanakill house, which was the residence of Mr. Hearn. It is labelled "Crotty's gun," and the
interest attached to it proves how the service must have been
estimated, in those days of imperfect police, of ridding the country of such a dreaded desperado.

At Crotty's trial, a woman, who lived with him as his wife,
appeared in court, in a state of pregnancy usually exhibited by
felons' female companions on such occasions; and when the
jury returned a verdict of guilty, and the judge was beginning
to pass sentence the criminal cried out, " A long day, my lord,
a long day." " I see no reason for granting it," said the judge.
" Oh, my lord," said the woman, " there is great reason, if it
was only to let him see the face of his child;" and she stood up
and exhibited her condition to the court. The request was
denied to the cruel felon, and he was executed next day. His
wife appeared at his wake, and her lament is recorded in a popular dirge, which is sung at this day, at wakes, in the county of
Tipperary. On the next page will be found the score of this
plaintive Irish melody, taken by a lady who often heard it sung
by the peasantry. The two first verses of the song commonly
appropriated to it are as follows :—

> " William Crotty I often tould you,
>   That David Norris would come round you,*
>   In your bed, when you lay sleeping,
>   And leave me here in sorrow weeping,
>   Och-hone, oh !

> " Oh, the judge but he was cruel,
>   Refused a long day to my jewel;
>   Sure I thought that you would, maybe,
>   See the face of your poor baby,
>   Och-hone, oh !"

Var. lect.—" Have sould you." But the reading in the text is correct; for
the Irish peasantry never regard the consonants in their rhymes.

CROTTY'S LAMENT.

Wil-liam Crot - ty, I of - ten tould you, That Da - vid Nor - ris would come round you, In your bed, when you lay sleep - - ing, And leave me here in sor - row weep - ing. Och - hone, och - hone, och - hone, oh!

Crotty was decapitated, according to his sentence, and his head was placed on a spike over the gate of the county gaol, which was at a great thoroughfare, and often a resting-place for those who brought milk to the markets. In a few days the head became in a state of putrid solution, and began to distil drops of gore into the milk-cans, for some time before it was discovered, to the inexpressible disgust and horror of all who had been drinking the milk. The hair did not decay with the flesh—it grew on the bony cranium; and there for a long time the ghastly skull of this miscreant excited as much horror after his death as his cruel actions had during his life.

When a criminal was executed for an offence for which his body was not liable to be given to the surgeons for dissection, his friends were allowed to take it. It was washed, and then laid on a truss of straw in a public street, with or without a head, and a plate was laid on the breast, with a halfpenny on it, as an invitation to passengers to contribute to the funeral. It formed sometimes a solemn spectacle, with the felon's widow at the head, wailing, with dishevelled hair, and singing, in a low dismal chant, her lament, her children ranged at the foot. But the utter indecency with which executions were then accompanied sometimes occasioned the most revolting and horrible scenes. About the same time at which the abominable occurrence just mentioned of Crotty's head took place, three highwaymen, Stackpole, Cashman, and Hierly, were hanged in Waterford. Their bodies were given to their friends, and were brought to the fish-house to be washed. While in the act of being washed, the bell rung to intimate a fresh arrival of fish; the bodies were hastily removed from the boards which they occupied, and the fish were thrown down in their place, swimming in the loathsome washings and blood of the corpses. The latter were then exposed on straw in the street, and an elderly gentleman, who communicated the circumstance, was brought by his nurse to see them, as a sight worthy of contemplation. The belief was, that if the beholder did not touch the body he saw, the ghost of it would haunt him; so he was led up by his nurse for the purpose, and laid his hands on them one after the other. The cold clammy feel and the ghastly spectacle never left his memory, but haunted him ever after.

To turn from such horrors, we will mention one more anecdote connected with the robberies of this period, which is perhaps the most singular in the annals of the detection of crime. At the close of the American war, Frederick Caulfield was on his way from England, when he met, in the ship, a young man named Hickey, and formed an acquaintance with him. They arrived in Waterford, and Hickey informed his companion that his friends lived in the county of Cork, and that he was going to see them, after a long absence in Newfoundland, where he had made some money, by the fishery, which he was carrying home; he invited Caulfield to accompany him, and they proceeded on their journey together. After a short time Caulfield came back to Waterford. He was a grave man, of decent appearance and serious, religious manners, and no observation was made on his returning alone. A trifling incident, however, drew attention to him. He wanted a dozen shirts made in a hurry, and to expedite them he gave them to twelve different sempstresses to work. Soon afterwards a rumour was heard of a young man who was expected home by his friends in Cork from Newfoundland, but had not appeared. On the circulation of this report, an innkeeper at Portlaw, named Rogers, came forward and stated that Caulfield had come to his house in company with Hickey, and left it along with him. On being asked if his house was not an inn much frequented, and if so, how he could swear to the identity of a casual passenger, whom he had never seen before, he hesitated, and said it was caused by a circumstance so extraordinary, that he was unwilling to mention it. On being pressed, he declared that on the morning of that day, his wife, on awaking, had told him a dream which had made a strong impression on her mind. Two men, she said, had entered the house together, dressed like sailors, a tall man and a short man; they had some refreshment, and soon after they left it. The spirit of her dream followed them, and she saw one of them strike the other as he descended a gap, murder him on the ground, rifle him, and bury him beside a hedge. The locality was distinctly painted to her vision, and she described the spot. As soon as Caulfield and Hickey entered the house she ran to her husband and said they were the men she had seen in her dream. They remained some time taking refreshment, eat and drank together in great apparent friendship, and, having obtained some directions as to their intended line of journey, they were about to depart, when Rogers, feeling some strong misgiving in his mind, from the impression his wife's dream had made upon him, entreated them to remain where they were till the morning. This they refused to do, and proceeded on their journey.

The locality described by Rogers as the scene of the murder in his wife's dream was searched. It was on the road between Portlaw and Carrick-on-Suir; and the body of Hickey was found there, in the identical situation indicated by the dream. Caulfield was arrested, tried at the ensuing assizes, and convicted. The circumstance of the dream being mentioned at the trial, the witnesses were cross-examined about it with a view to throw ridicule on their testimony; but the manner in which it had transpired before the finding of the body made a deep impression on the jury. The judge, whose name, by a curious coincidence, was also Caulfield, in passing sentence, strongly adverted to it as an instance of the interference of Providence for the detection of murder.

Caulfield, after conviction, acknowledged his guilt. He said that the steady gaze of the innkeeper's wife, as he entered the inn at Portlaw, so appalled him, that he had given up the design of murdering his companion, till he himself afforded him an opportunity. He had a stick which hurt his hand, and Hickey offered him his knife to pare it. He was in the act of doing so, and Hickey was descending a gap in the hedge, when " the devil," said Caulfield, "appeared to me, and whispered in my ear, ' now strike.' " He did so, then cut Hickey's throat with his own knife while he lay on the ground, robbed him, and tried to bury him in the spot where he was found. Another remarkable circumstance connected with the dream was the mode of its interpretation. The dream represented the less of the two men murdering the larger; this was contrary to the fact; but that was

" Confirmation strong as proof of holy writ,"

to demonstrate the truth of the vision, to those who believed in dreams then in Ireland—the established faith being that dreams always go by contraries.*

Caulfield's confession and appearance of sincere penitence, coupled with the mysterious discovery of his guilt, interested many of the religious in Waterford in his favour. Several persons of great respectability and high connexions visited him daily in prison, for devotional purposes. He was a handsome man, and particularly attentive to his dress. The ladies therefore purchased different articles, which they sent, for him to choose the most becoming to die in; and when the hour for the last awful scene approached, a large company, particularly ladies, were admitted at the gaol, and formed a long procession. The place of execution was then about a mile out of the town, and they walked with the murderer to the foot of the gallows, chanting the fifty-first psalm, in which he appeared to join with fervent piety. Such an extraordinary spectacle at a public execution is hardly less striking than—though so strong a contrast to—the horrible levities that often followed such scenes sixty years ago.

CHAPTER X.

TIGER ROCHE.

AMONG the characters distinguished for unbridled indulgence and fierce passions, who were, unfortunately, too frequently to

---

* A curious illustration of this—in Ireland almost universal—superstition, occurred in the reign of Elizabeth. The Earl of Leicester and Duke of Ormond were deadly enemies, and the latter denounced the former as a villain and a coward. This coming to Leicester's ears, he met Ormond in the ante-chamber at court, and, after saluting him with apparent courtesy, said; "I was dreaming of you last night." Ormond asked what was the dream. "I dreamed," said the Earl, "that I gave you a box on the ear." "Very good," replied the Duke of Ormond; "and as dreams always go by contraries, that portends that *I* must box *you*," and struck him a blow in the face. For this offence Ormond was imprisoned, but insisted he was only accomplishing Leicester's dream. He was soon afterwards liberated.

be met with in Ireland in the last century, was one whose name attained so much celebrity as to become a proverb. "Tiger Roche," as he was called, was a native of Dublin, where he was born in the year 1729. He received the best education the metropolis could afford, and was instructed in all the accomplishments then deemed essential to the rank and character of a gentleman. So expert was he in the various acquirements of polite life, that at the age of sixteen he recommended himself to Lord Chesterfield, then Lord Lieutenant of Ireland, who offered him, gratuitously, a commission in the army; but his friends having other views for him, they declined it. This seems to have been a serious misfortune to the young man, whose disposition and education strongly inclined him to a military life. His hopes were raised, and his vanity flattered, by the notice and offer of the viceroy; and in sullen resentment he absolutely refused to embark in any other profession his friends designed for him. He continued, therefore, for several years among the dissipated idlers of the metropolis, having no laudable pursuit to occupy his time, and led into all the outrages and excesses which then disgraced Dublin.

One night in patrolling the city with his drunken associates, they attacked and killed a watchman, who, with others, had attempted to quell a riot they had excited. He was, therefore, compelled to fly from Dublin. He made his way to Cork, where he lay concealed for some time, and from thence escaped to the plantations in North America. When the war broke out between France and England, he entered as a volunteer in one of the provincial regiments, and distinguished himself in several engagements with the Indians in the interest of the French, during which he seems to have acquired those fierce and cruel qualities by which those tribes are distinguished.

He was now particularly noticed by his officers for the intrepidity and spirit he displayed, and was high in favour with Colonel Massy, his commander; but an accident occurred of so humiliating and degrading a nature, as to extinguish at once all his hopes of advancement. An officer of Massy's regiment was possessed of a very valuable fowling-piece which he highly prized. He missed it from his tent, and made diligent inquiry after it, but it was nowhere to be found. It was, however, reported that it was seen in the possession of Roche, and an order was made to examine his baggage. On searching among it the lost article was found. Roche declared that he had bought it from one Bourke, a countryman of his own, and a corporal in his regiment. Bourke was sent for and examined. He solemnly declared on oath that the statement of Roche was altogether false, and that he himself knew nothing at all of the transaction. Roche was now brought to a court-martial, and little appearing in his favour, he was convicted of the theft, and, as a lenient punishment, ordered to quit the service with every mark of disgrace and ignominy. Irritated with this treatment, Roche immediately challenged the officer who had prosecuted him. He refused, however, to meet him, on the pretext that he was a degraded man, and no longer entitled to the rank and consideration of a gentleman. Stung to madness, and no longer master of himself, he rushed to the parade, insulted the officer in the grossest terms, and then flew to the picket-guard, where he attacked the corporal with his naked sword, declaring his intention to kill him on the spot. The man with difficulty defended his life, till his companions sprung upon Roche and disarmed him. Though deprived of his weapon, he did not desist from his intention ; crouching down like an Indian foe, he suddenly sprung, like Rhoderick Dhu, at his antagonist, and fastened on his throat with his teeth, and before he could be disengaged nearly strangled him, dragging away a mouthful of flesh, which, in the true Indian spirit, he afterwards said, was " the sweetest morsel he had ever tasted." From the fierce and savage character he displayed on this occasion, he obtained the appellation of " Tiger," an affix which was ever after joined to his name.

A few days after, the English army advanced to force the lines of Ticonderaga. Unfortunate Roche was left desolate and alone in the wilderness, an outcast from society, apparently abandoned by all the world. His resolution and fidelity to his cause, however, did not desert him. He pursued his way through the woods till he fell in with a party of friendly Indians, and by extraordinary exertions and forced marches, arrived at the fortress with his Indians, to join in the attack. He gave distinguished proofs of his courage and military abilities during that unfortunate affair, and received four dangerous wounds. He attracted the notice of General Abercrombie, the leader of the expedition; but the stain of robbery was upon him, and no services, however brilliant, could obliterate it.

From hence he made his way to New York, after suffering incredible afflictions from pain, poverty, and sickness. One man alone, Governor Rogers, pitied his case, and was not satisfied of his guilt. In the year 1785, Roche received from his friends in Ireland a reluctant supply of money, which enabled him to obtain a passage on board a vessel bound for England, where he arrived shortly afterwards. He reserved part of his supply of money for the purchase of a commission, and hoped once more to ascend to that rank from which he had been, as he thought, unjustly degraded; but just as the purchase was about to be completed, a report of his theft in America reached the regiment, and the officers refused to serve with him. With great perseverance and determined resolution, he traced the origin of the report to a Captain Campbell, then residing at the British Coffee-house, in Charing-cross. He met him in the public room, taxed him with what he called a gross and false calumny, which the other retorted with great spirit. A duel immediately ensued, in which both were desperately wounded.

Roche now declared in all public places, and caused it to be everywhere known, that, as he could not obtain justice on the miscreant who had traduced his character in America, he would personally chastise every man in England who presumed to propagate the report. With this determination, he met one day, in the Green Park, his former colonel, Massy, and another officer, who had just returned home. He addressed them, and anxiously requested they would, as they might, remove the stain from his character. They treated his appeal with contempt, when he fiercely attacked them both. They immediately drew their swords, and disarmed him. A crowd of spectators assembled round, and being two to one they inflicted severe chastisement on Roche. Foiled in his attempt, he immediately determined to seek another occasion, and finding that one of them had departed for Chester, Roche set out after him with the indefatigable perseverance and pursuit of a bloodhound. Here Roche again sought him, and meeting him in the streets, again attacked him. Roche was, however, again defeated, and received a severe wound in the sword-arm, which long disabled him.

But that redress to his character now came accidentally and unexpectedly, which all his activity and perseverance could not obtain. Bourke, the corporal, was mortally wounded by a scalping party of Indians, and on his death-bed made a solemn confession that he himself had actually stolen the fowling-piece, and sold it to Roche, without informing him by what means he had procured it, and that Roche had really purchased it without any suspicion of the theft. This declaration of the dying man was properly attested, and universally received, and restored the injured Roche at once to character and countenance. His former calumniators now vied with each other in friendly offers to serve him; and as a remuneration for the injustice and injury he had suffered, a lieutenancy in a newly-raised regiment was conferred upon him gratuitously. He soon returned to Dublin with considerable eclat; the reputation of the injuries he had sustained, the gallant part he had acted, and the romantic adventures he had encountered among the Indians, in the woods of America, were the subject of every conversation. Convivial parties were everywhere made for him. Wherever he appeared, he was the lion of the night. A handsome person, made still more attractive by the wounds he had received, a graceful form in the dance, in which he excelled, and the narrative of "his hair-breadth 'scapes," with which he was never too diffident to indulge the company, made him at this time "the observed of all observers" in the metropolis of Ireland.

But a service which he rendered the public in Dublin

deservedly placed him very high in their esteem and good-will. It was at this time infested with those miscreants whom we have before mentioned, "sweaters," or "pinkindindies," and every night some outrage was perpetrated on the peace-able and unoffending inhabitants. One evening late, an old gentleman with his son and daughter, were returning home from a friend's house, when they were attacked on Ormond-quay by a party of them. Roche, who was accidentally going the same way at the same time, heard the shrieks of a woman crying for assistance, and instantly rushed to the place. Here he did not hesitate singly to meet the whole party. He first rescued the young woman from the ruffian who held her, and then attacking the band, he desperately wounded some, and put the rest to flight. His spirited conduct on this occasion gained him a high and deserved reputation, and inspired others with resolution to follow his example. He formed a body, consisting of officers and others of his acquaintance, to patrol the dangerous streets of Dublin at night, and so gave that pro-tection to the citizens which the miserable and decrepit watch were not able to afford.

But he was not fated long to preserve the high character he had acquired. His physical temperament, impossible to manage, and his moral perceptions, hard to regulate, were the sport of every contingency and vicissitude of fortune. The peace concluded in 1763 reduced the army, and he retired in indigent circumstances to London, where he soon lived beyond his income. In order to repair it, he paid his addresses to a Miss Pitt, who had a fortune of £4,000. On the anticipation of this, he engaged in a career of extravagance that soon ac-cumulated debts to a greater amount, and the marriage portion was insufficient to satisfy his creditors. He was arrested and cast into the prison of the King's Bench, where various de-tainers were laid upon him, and he was doomed to a confine-ment of hopeless termination. Here his mind appears to have been completely broken down, and the intrepid and daring courage, which had sustained him in so remarkable a manner through all the vicissitudes of his former life, seemed to be totally exhausted. He submitted to insults and indignities with patience, and seemed deprived not only of the capability to resent, but of the sensibility to feel them.

On one occasion he had a trifling dispute with a fellow-prisoner, who kicked him, and struck him a blow in the face. There was a time when his fiery spirit would not have been satisfied but with the blood of the offender. He now only turned aside and cried like a child. It happened that his countryman, Buck English, whom we have before noticed, was confined at the same time in the Bench; with him also he had some dispute, and English, seizing a stick, flogged him in a savage manner. Roche made no attempt to retaliate or resist, but crouched under the punishment. But while he shrunk thus under the chastisement of men, he turned upon his wife, whom he treated with such cruelty, that she was compelled to separate from him, and abandon him to his fate.

At length, however, an act of grace liberated him from a confinement under which all his powers were fast sinking; and a small legacy, left him by a relation, enabled him once more to appear in the gay world. With his change of fortune a change of disposition came over him; and in proportion as he had shown an abject spirit in confinement, he now exhibited even a still more arrogant and irritable temper than he had ever before displayed. He was a constant frequenter of billiard-tables, where he indulged an insufferable assumption, with sometimes a shrewd and keen remark. He was one day driving the balls about with the cue, and on some one expostulating with him that he was not playing himself, but hindering other gentlemen from their amusement; " Gentlemen!" said Roche, " why, sir, except you and I, and one or two more, there is not a gentleman in the room." His friend afterwards remarked that he had grossly offended a large company, and wondered some of them had not resented the affront. " Oh!" said Roche, " there was no fear of that. There was not a thief in the room that did not consider himself *one* of the *two* or *three* gentlemen I excepted."

Again his fortune seemed in the ascendant, and the miserable, spiritless, flogged and degraded prisoner of the King's Bench was called on to stand as candidate to represent Middlesex in Parliament. So high an opinion was entertained of his daring spirit, that it was thought by some of the popular party he might be of use in intimidating Colonel Luttrell, who was the declared opponent of Wilkes at that election. In April, 1769, he was put into nomination at Brentford by Mr. Jones, and seconded by Mr. Martin, two highly popular electors. He, however, disappointed his friends, and declined the poll, induced, it was said, by promises of Luttrell's friends to provide for him. On this occasion he fought another duel with a Captain Flood, who had offended him in a coffee-house. He showed no deficiency of courage, but on the contrary even a larger proportion of spirit and generosity than had distinguished him at former periods.

Returning at this time one night to his apartments at Chelsea, he was attacked by two ruffians, who presented pistols to his breast. He sprang back, and drew his sword, when one of them fired at him, and the ball grazed his temple. He then attacked them both, pinned one to the wall, and the other fled. Roche secured his prisoner, and the other was apprehended next day. They were tried at the Old Bailey, and capitally convicted; but at the humane and earnest intercession of Roche, their punishment was mitigated to transportation.

All the fluctuations of this strange man's character seemed at length to settle into one unhappy state, from which he was unable ever again to raise himself. He met with a young person, walking with her mother in St. James's Park, and was struck with her appearance. He insinuated himself into their acquaintance, and the young lady formed for him a strong and uncontrollable attachment. She possessed a considerable fortune, of which Roche became the manager. His daily profusion and dissipation soon exhausted her property, and the mother and daughter were compelled to leave London, reduced to indigence and distress, in consequence of the debts in which he had involved them.

He was soon after appointed captain of a company of foot in the East India service, and embarked in the Vansittart, for India, in May, 1773. He had not been many days on board, when such was his impracticable temper that he fell out with

all the passengers, and among the rest with a Captain Ferguson, who called him out as soon as they arrived at Madeira.
Roche was again seized with a sudden and unaccountable fit
of terror, and made submission.   The arrogance and cowardice
he displayed revolted the whole body of the passengers, and
they unanimously made it a point that the captain should
expel him from the table.   He was driven, therefore, to the
society of the common sailors and soldiers on board the ship.
With them he endeavoured to ingratiate himself, by mixing
freely with them, and denouncing vengeance against every
gentleman and officer on board the ship; but his threats were
particularly directed against Ferguson, whom he considered
the origin of the disgrace he suffered.   On the arrival of the
ship at the Cape, after all the passengers were disembarked,
Roche came ashore, in the dusk of the evening, and was seen
about the door of the house where Ferguson lodged.   A message was conveyed to Ferguson, who went out, and was found
soon afterwards round the corner of the house, weltering in his
blood, with *nine* deep wounds, all on his left side; and it was
supposed they must have been there inflicted, because it was
the unprotected side, and the attack was made when he was off
his guard.

Suspicion immediately fixed on Roche as the murderer; he
fled during the night, and took refuge among the Caffres.   It
was supposed that he ended his strange and eventful life soon
after.   The Cape was at that time a colony of the Dutch, who,
vigilant and suspicious of strangers, suffered none to enter
there, but merely to touch for provisions and pass on.   The
proceedings, therefore, of their colonial government were shut
up in mystery.   It was reported at the time, that Roche was
demanded and given up to the authorities of the Cape, who
caused him to be broken alive upon the wheel, according to
the then Dutch criminal law of the Cape, which inflicted that
punishment on the more atrocious murderers, and the uncer-
tainty that hung about the circumstance assorted strangely
with the wild character of the man.

It appears, however, he was tried by the Dutch authorities
at the Cape, and acquitted.   He then took a passage in a

French vessel to Bombay; but the Vansittart, in which he had
come from England to the Cape, had arrived in India before
him; information had been given to the British authorities,
charging Roche with Ferguson's murder; and Roche was
arrested as soon as he landed. He urged his right to be discharged, or at least bailed, on the grounds that there was not
sufficient evidence against him; that he had been already acquitted; and that as the offence, if any, was committed out of
the British dominions, he could only be tried by special commission, and it was uncertain whether the Crown would issue
one or not, or, if the Crown did grant a commission, when or
where it would sit. He argued his own case with the skill of
a practised lawyer. The authorities, however, declined either
to bail or discharge him, and he was kept in custody until he
was sent a prisoner to England, to stand his trial.

An appeal of murder was brought against him, and a commission issued to try it. The case came on at the Old Bailey,
in London, before Baron Burland, on the 11th December,
1775. The counsel for Roche declined in any way relying on
the former acquittal at the Cape of Good Hope; and the case
was again gone through. The fact of the killing was undis-
puted, but from the peculiar nature of the proceedings, there
could not be, as in a common indictment for murder, a conviction for manslaughter; and the judge directed the jury, if they
did not believe the killing to be malicious and deliberate,
absolutely to acquit the prisoner. The jury brought in a verdict of acquittal.

The doubt about Roche's guilt arose on the following state
of facts. On the evening of their arrival at the Cape, Ferguson and his friends were sitting at tea, at their lodgings, when
a message was brought into the room; on hearing which Ferguson rose, went to his apartment, and, having put on his
sword and taken a loaded cane in his hand, went out. A
friend named Grant followed him, and found Roche and him
at the side of the house, round a corner, and heard the clash of
swords, but refused to interfere. It was too dark to see what
was occurring; but in a few moments he heard Roche going
away, and Ferguson falling. Ferguson was carried in, and

died immediately. All his wounds were in the *left* side. The most violent vindictive feelings had existed between them; and there was proof of Roche's having threatened "to shorten the race of the Fergusons." The message, in answer to which Ferguson went out, was differently stated, being, according to one account, "Mr. Mathews wants Mr. Ferguson," and to the other, "a gentleman wants Mr. Mathews." The case for the prosecution was, that this message was a trap to draw Ferguson out of the house, and that, on his going out, Roche attacked him; and this was confirmed by the improbability of Roche's going out for an innocent purpose, in a strange place, on the night of his landing, in the dark, and in the neighbourhood of Ferguson's lodgings; and particularly by the wounds being on the left side, which they could not be if given in a fair fight with small swords. Roche's account was, that on the evening of his arrival he went out to see the town, accompanied by a boy, a slave of his host; that they were watched by some person till they came near Ferguson's, when that person disappeared, and immediately afterwards, Roche was struck with a loaded stick on the head, knocked down, and his arm disabled; that afterwards he succeeded in rising, and, perceiving Ferguson, drew his sword, and after a struggle, in which he wished to avoid bloodshed, killed his assailant in self-defence. This was, to some extent, corroborated by the boy at the Dutch trial, and by a sailor in England, but both these witnesses were shaken a little in their testimony. According to this account, the message was a concerted signal to Ferguson, who had set a watch on Roche, intending to assassinate him. The locality of Ferguson's wounds was accounted for by his fighting both with cane and sword, using the former to parry. If the second version of the message was correct it would strongly confirm this account. There was no proof that Ferguson knew any one named Mathews.

A writer of the last century, in speaking of the Irish character, concludes with the remark:—" In short, if they are good, you will scarcely meet a better: if bad, you will seldom find a worse." These extremes were frequently mixed in the same person. Roche, at different periods, displayed them. At one time, an admirable spirit, great humanity, and unbounded generosity; at another, abject cowardice, ferocity, treachery, and brutal selfishness. The vicissitudes of his fortune were as variable as his character: at times he was exposed to the foulest charges, and narrowly escaped ignominious punishment; at others he was the object of universal esteem and admiration.

CHAPTER XI.

THE KINGDOM OF DALKEY—THE DALKEY GAZETTE— T. O'MEARA.

AMONG the singular societies which have existed in Ireland within the last sixty years, was the "Kingdom of Dalkey and its Officers." It was then common, in forming associations, serious or convivial, to adopt, instead of the plebeian name of "club," some more high-sounding title. A society of gentlemen, who established a court of honour to suppress duelling, by the contradictory expedient of making themselves such excellent swordsmen that all others would be afraid to fight with them, called themselves the "Knights of Tara." They originally named themselves the Knights of St. Patrick; but on the institution of that illustrious order, in 1783, by the crown, the anti-duellists changed their title. The latter illustrious order (of Knights of St. Patrick) was founded in compliment to the national feeling, after the establishment of the independence of the Irish legislature. A little later in date, but in retrospective commemoration of the same great event, was founded the Kingdom of Dalkey.

The Kingdom of Dalkey consisted of a small island which lies on the south side of the bay of Dublin, opposite the now populous town bearing the same name. The district then presented a very different appearance from what it does now. There were then no railroads, no taverns, no cottages, no villas, scarcely even a fisherman's cabin, on the solitary shore. One

small tavern stood on a promontory at Dunleary, occasionally
visited by collegians on a Sunday for breakfast, where the
primitive fare supplied was a wash-hand basin of sea-gull and
other eggs, and a large dish of fried flounders. With the
exception of this eccentric hostelry, and the two little collections
of cabins then forming the towns of Dalkey and Dunleary, the
entire was a deserted waste, till the traveller returned to the
Blackrock, then the Ultima Thule of the Dublin citizens. The
part immediately opposite the island was called " Dalkey Stone
Common ;" and the ground, which is now eagerly rented at
the foot and inch by money-making builders, was then tenanted
by the acre by a few roaming asses. It would be difficult to
find any two places presenting so great a contrast as " Dalkey
as it was," even so short a time since, and " Dalkey as it is."

Dalkey is not, however, without its historic recollections,
but of a much more ancient period than its royal state. On
the island there are the remains of a small chapel, dedicated to
its patron saint, St. Benedict. The chapel has been in ruins for
many centuries. About it were formerly some kistvaens, or
stone coffins, and human bones, of which they had been the
receptacles. From its seclusion, and the communication with
the mainland being cut off by Dalkey Sound, it was selected as
a safe retreat during the epidemic diseases which formerly
ravaged Ireland. In the great plague which visited Dublin in
1575, the citizens retreated there, and the island was covered
with the tents of the refugees while the sickness continued.
From the shelter afforded by the island, Dalkey was anciently
thought a commodious substitute for a harbour ; and several
eminent persons are recorded to have landed or embarked
there. Sir A. St. Leger, Lord Deputy, in 1540, and Sir W.
Skeffington, in 1534, on their way to Dublin, and in 1414, Sir
John Talbot, afterwards Lord Furnival, Lord Lieutenant of
Ireland, landed there. In 1558, Lord Sussex embarked there
to oppose the Scottish invaders at Rathlin, on the coast of
Antrim. There are several ruined castles—the castles of Bullock—in the immediate neighbourhood ; and when they were
built, the place must have been of some importance. It had a
charter, and there were markets held there about the year 1500,

and the castles were intended as stores to protect the merchan-
dise from pirates; but for centuries the castles have been ruins,
and, since 1600, the trading town of Dalkey dwindled into a few
miserable fishermen's huts. There was formerly established,
at some distance inland, the Dalkey cotton factory, which was
one of the earliest, if not the earliest cotton-factory worked in
Ireland. It belonged to a Mr. Costelloe, but was burned down
in 1781.

Notwithstanding its historic recollections, the shore was, until
within the last twenty-five years, the most secluded and desolate
part of the bay of Dublin; and the little uninhabited island, of
course, still more solitary. Its only inhabitants were a few
wild rabbits, until it was colonized by the Irish government, in
1804, with a couple of artillerymen. In the summer of 1779,
when the descent of the French on Bantry Bay was generally
expected, rumours of their having actually landed were con-
stantly going abroad. The papers in opposition to the government ridiculed and made light of the alarm. Among the
popular squibs published with this object, were cautions against
their making a descent on Dalkey, and a proposal to fortify the
island to prevent their landing, and Bagotrath Castle to inter-
cept their march to Dublin. The latter was a ruined castle at
the end of Baggot Street, the government of which was a sine-
cure office. The writer of the squib little thought that his
proposal would be seriously acted on by the Irish parliament.
Bagotrath Castle has been pulled down, and its place is occupied by a handsome street; but the island of Dalkey has been
actually fortified to defend us against the French, and an
absurd martello tower and battery stand there to this day.
They form an agreeable fishing-lodge for two artillerymen, and
a depot of plates for pic-nic parties on the island; but are not
likely ever to answer any more useful object.

The convivial society,* of which the King of Dalkey was
the president, was carried on with a degree of spirit, and
attracted a portion of public attention not easily imagined in

* Some notice of this society, as well as of a few other particulars mentioned
in the preceding chapters, may be found in "Herbert's Irish Varieties"—a book
which the writer regrets he did not see till long after the matter of this volume
was published.

the present tame state of society. They met once in each year on the island. The king was elective, and the professed object of the visit was that he might resign his crown into the hands of his subjects, and a new election be had. There was a paper then published in Dublin called "The Morning Post, or Dublin Courant." It was printed by a man named Cooney, and devoted a column to the proceedings of the society, under the heading of the "Dalkey Gazette." The day of the intended ceremony on the island was duly announced in the Dalkey Gazette, in the form of a proclamation from the king, and the arrangements and ceremonies to be observed officially advertised by the chamberlain. The party usually proceeded from Dublin by water; and the solitary island and neighbouring shore became a scene of great bustle and gaiety, and were crowded by thousands of spectators.

The day selected was a Sunday in the end of August or beginning of September. The general outline of the proceedings was as follows:—The king landed in state, and was saluted by firing shots on the island. He assembled the most convivial members of the society under the names of his principal officers, and the other guests as his subjects, and, in a mock heroic speech, resigned his crown into their hands, and desired them to elect a successor. A re-election always followed, and his majesty, in a second speech, expressed his gratitude, was anointed with a bottle of whiskey, and crowned among the plaudits of the people. He then received their petitions and complaints, which were tendered and spoken upon with comic gravity. The members were all of the popular side in politics, and the entire proceeding was made the groundwork for squibs on the political topics of the day. Then followed a sermon from the chief of the Druids and primate of Dalkey, preached in the ruined church, which was called the Cathedral of Dalkey. This latter proceeding was often not a little objectionable, in treating with levity sacred subjects. An ode composed for the occasion was then sung by all the people, and the whole ceremony concluded by a feast on the rocks, after which his majesty and his officers of state again embarked in pomp, and were followed by his people.

The last president of this curious society was a convivial Dublin bookseller, named Armitage, who reigned under the title of " King Stephen the First." There is a cluster of rocks near Dalkey called the Muglins, and another called the Maiden; there are also some small islands—one called Magee, in the bay, and the others, Ireland's Eye and Lambay, on the north of Howth. The king's title united dignities derived from all these localities, in the following form :—His facetious Majesty, Stephen the First, King of Dalkey, Emperor of the Muglins, Prince of the Holy Island of Magee, and Elector of Lambay and Ireland's Eye, Defender of his own Faith, and respecter of all others, Sovereign of the illustrious order of the Lobster and Periwinkle." Another illustrious member was " My Lord Tokay," a wine-merchant. The office of primate was filled by a Mr. Gillespie. Beside filling the columns of the " Dalkey Gazette," the proceedings of the society attracted so much attention, and were considered to be conducted with so much humour and cleverness, that their annual meetings were recorded in most of the Dublin papers among the remarkable news of the day.

The politics of " Cooney's Morning Post " were very democratic, and the " Dalkey Gazette " of course was of the same tone. Its merit consisted in being a serio-comic record of the proceedings of the society, and in satirizing the political events of the day, by means of this mimic kingdom—much in the style of a Christmas pantomime. It must have been indebted for its popularity greatly to the feelings of its readers. The paper is now difficult to be met with; and we give the following extract as a specimen. It is from the " Dalkey Gazette " of September 10, 1792, and will give an idea of its general character. It appeared in " Cooney's Post " of September 22.

To understand its point, it is necessary to bear in mind what were the political topics of the day. It was the year of the most violent proceedings in the French revolution. In the preceding month, the King of France had been dethroned, and was then a prisoner in the hands of the Paris populace. Even the most just and rational propositions respecting civil liberty were dreaded by the ultra loyal, as indications of revolutionary

principles; and not without reason, as they were most frequently in the mouths of persons who used them merely as
introductory to more dangerous doctrines. The popular topic
in Ireland was the "Catholic claims;" and the Chancellor,
Fitzgibbon, had made himself peculiarly odious to the Roman
Catholics, by his declaration that their meetings to petition for
a redress of grievances were unconstitutional and illegal.
Among other bodies, the Dublin Corporation had also incurred
their hostility by its declaration in favour of Protestant ascendancy. The radical papers of the day teemed with charges of
the corruption of the government and their subordinates; and
some of them—particularly the "Morning Post"—broadly
insinuated that £20,000 of the public money was missing,
through the default of the Chancellor of the Exchequer, Sir J.
Parnell. Lord Westmoreland was the Lord Lieutenant; and
his parsimony and want of hospitality at the Castle were popular subjects of attack. All these topics appear to have been
alluded to at the coronation of his facetious majesty in this year.

The "Gazette" commences with a description in mock
heroics of the voyage from Ringsend to Dalkey, during which
his Dalkian majesty saluted two ships of his Britannic majesty,
which duly returned the compliment. It details the offerings
of his majesty's faithful subjects from Lambay and the holy
knights of Magee, consisting of rabbits, cockles, and mushrooms;
and describes the ceremony of the resignation and coronation
as follows:—

"His majesty held a levee at the palace, at which were
present several of the nobility of the empire, and a great number of illustrious foreigners from Bullock, Dunleary, Howth,
and other parts of the neighbouring continent. His majesty
then ascended the great rock—the senate-house where the
states of the empire were assembled—and being led to the foot
of the throne by the chancellor and primate, and preceded by
the lord mayor, as representing the municipality of Dalkey,
his majesty declined ascending the royal seat; but, turning
round to the assembly, and putting off his royal diadem, he
laid it, with his oaken sceptre, on the table, and addressed the
assembly:—

" ' My lords, gentlemen, and citizens of Dalkey, I am come this day to commemorate, with my cheerful people, the occasion which raised me to the throne of this realm. I rejoice exceedingly that nothing like hereditary pretensions are quoted in my escutcheon, or ranked among my claims to that dignity, which I hold, not as an inheritance from ancestors who attained it by injustice, rapine, and bloodshed, but that I enjoy it by the most honourable of all claims,—the choice, confidence, and affections of a free, generous, and happy people. It is my glory that I love you all, my pride to have you happy, and my joy that you think so. To manifest my sincerity, I wish to establish in the happy constitution of Dalkey the principle which places its liberty and happiness above the power of permanent tyrants, and depositing in the people the controlling discretion,' " &c.

His majesty proceeded in the same strain at some length, and ended by resigning his regal authority, and desiring his subjects to select a successor, concluding with the following sentiment—

" ' I am not an advocate for the prerogative of kings against the rights of the race of Adam. My ambition was always to reign over your hearts and affections, and not above your liberties.'

" The lord chancellor, in a speech of considerable length, disadvised his majesty from soliciting that which must ever circumscribe the rights attached to the crown of Dalkey, and resigning that ' penance from power, prerogative, and patronage' which his predecessors had maintained with dignity, regardless of the notions of that long-eared mobocracy called the people."

His majesty made another rather dull political address, and insisted on resigning; after which—

" The viceroy of Ireland's Eye, King of Arms, went forth preceded by a herald, and proclaimed the king's resignation, and demanded of the people to nominate a king from the great body of the natives whom they would choose to rule over them. The whole, with one voice, named their beloved monarch, Stephen the First. His facetious majesty was then again crowned ; and after taking the oaths of festivity and public justice on a bowl of grog, was again proclaimed king.

" Lord Minikin, Keeper of the Tower, by order of his majesty, then went forth, and proclaimed that his majesty, in open senate, was ready to hear the complaints, and grant the just desires of his people.

" A deputation from the Order of the Periwinkle immediately came to the bar of the assembly, and presented articles of impeachment against the lord chancellor—first, for corruption in his official capacity ; secondly, for violating the solemn obligations taken when he was appointed one of his facetious majesty's most honourable privy council ; thirdly, mal-administration of justice ; fourthly, his late unconstitutional conduct in using undue influence, as a peer of the realm, at a meeting of the Order of the Scallop, to make them declare, contrary to the known laws of the empire, that the members of the Periwinkle had not a right, individually and collectively, to petition the king and senate for a redress of grievances."

The chancellor makes an affidavit of the absence of several material witnesses, who consist of certain unpopular members of the Dublin corporation, and his trial is adjourned. An impeachment is then exhibited against Lord Glasthule, Tony Laughable, Lord Mayor of Dalkey, and the Lord Chancellor, as guardians of the realm, for neglecting inquiring into the interior departments of the kingdom, whereby his majesty's subjects were oppressed, good humour and harmony interrupted, and his majesty's revenues impaired. The Committee of Finance also exhibited articles of impeachment against the Lords of the Treasury for embezzlement of £20,000, good gingerbread money of the realm.

These are ordered to stand over ; and after some more popular speeches on the foundation of a new order called " The Virtuous Citizen," the festivities are detailed as follows :—

" His majesty retired to a sumptuous banquet ; the lord mayor and municipality perambulated the franchises. They were met at Stony-gate by a party of the Liberty boys of Dalkey, who, according to custom, took the sword from his lordship's sword-bearer. At the great mole his lordship threw the civic dart into the sea, and then returned to the civic hall, and partook of a sumptuous repast, in the course of which a plenipotentiary arrived from the Grand Duke of Bullock, with a present of potatoes, ready boiled, which his majesty graciously accepted, and conferred the honour of knighthood on the ambassador."

Songs were sung, thanks returned, and toasts drank, and the whole concluded with a ball on the island, all of which are detailed in the " Gazette," in the same mock serious style. The favourite toasts drank on the occasion were such as " May the will of the people be the law of the land ;" " Equal liberty, civil and religious, to all sons of Adam," &c.

This " Gazette" contains a very long political sermon, supposed to be delivered by the primate on the occasion of the coronation. The sermon inculcates many admirable lessons of liberality, generosity, and justice ; bnt the vein of levity with which it imitates sacred doctrines and texts is often very objectionable, to say nothing of the abuse and misrepresentation of the clerical character which it conveys. It seems to be an elaborate composition, and to have been prized by the editor of the " Morning Post," who introduces it twice into his paper, apparently as a serious political article. A considerable part of it is occupied by commendations of hospitality and good fellowship, and condemnations of their opposites, made with obvious allusion to the lord lieutenant. The following may be taken as a specimen :—

" The gay flowrets of cheerfulness, the balm of friendship, the jessamine of taste, the myrtle of love, or the sweet rose of justice, never take root in his dull and barren soul. The rue of envy, the abortive savin of distrust, the rank hemlock of murky avarice, and the deadly nightshade of chill penury, are the native vegetables of that ungenial soil."

And the following blessing :—

" The blessing of the beggar and the clerk of the crown attend you in all your adventures in this life, and the last prayer of the recorder and of all the judges of the crown circuit attend you in the next."

In 1796, when political prosecutions were numerous, the government were not very scrupulous in the means of obtaining evidence.　Toler was the solicitor-general, and had gone as a judge of assize, and tried several of the state prisoners.　Toler's well-known failings and the government policy are noted in the Dalkey proceedings as follows:—

" The second sergeant was accused of making puns from the bench as arguments against the prisoner's life; but being absent in another kingdom to fight a duel, he could not appear to answer for himself.

" The opinion of the lawyers was, that evidence obtained by force ought not to attaint the blood of any subject of Dalkey."

The odes composed for these commemmorations had various degrees of merit.　The following are three verses of the ode of 1793 :—

> " If sprung from woman, say,
>   Did you first know the day,
>   Without a shirt ?
>   Or must you, like the clown,
>   Spite of your great renown,
>   Lay your great body down,
>   Deep in the dirt ?
>
> " Lord of all Dalkey lands,
>   Chief of your jovial bands,
>   Are you not man ?
>   With you though peace doth reign,
>   Nor blood your isle doth stain,
>   Nor famine here complain,
>   Are you not man ?
>
> " What though the realms rejoice
>   In your melodious voice :
>   Kings are but men !
>   And while each subject sings :
>   ' God made us men, not kings !'
>   With echo Dalkey rings :
>   ' Kings are but men !' "

The last meeting of the society was held on the 20th of August, 1797.　It was the year immediately preceding the breaking out of the rebellion, and the gaols were filled with prisoners accused of treason.　The greater part of the country was treated as under martial law, and the soldiers were living at free quarters to assist the sheriffs.　The United Irishmen were the great object of suspicion to the government.　The

mutiny at the Nore had ended only a month previously. The
Dalkey meeting appears to have been more loyal than usual.
The toasts were, " the King," "the Army," &c. The following
is an extract from the ode of the year. It is believed to be
from the pen of T. Moore, who was a faithful and most convivial subject of his facetious majesty, and it is interesting as one
of Moore's earliest poetic efforts:—

> " Hail, happy Dalkey, Queen of Isles,
> Where justice reigns and freedom smiles.
>
> In Dalkey Justice holds her state,
> Unaided by the prison gate ;
> No subjects of King Stephen lie
> In loathsome cells, they know not why ;
> Health, peace, and good humour, in music's soft strains,
> Invite and UNITE us in Dalkey's wide plains.
>
> " No flimsy sheriff enters here ;
> No trading justice dare appear ;
> No soldier asks his comrade whether
> The sheriff has yet cleaned his feather ;
> Our soldiers here deserve the name :
> Nor wear a feather they don't pluck from fame.
>
> " How much unlike those wretched realms,
> Where wicked statesmen guide the helms ;
> Here no first-rate merchants breaking ;
> Here no first-rate vessels taking ;
> Here no property is shaking ;
> Here no shameful peace is making ;
> Here we snap no apt occasion
> On the pretext of invasion ;
> Here informers get no pensions
> To requite their foul inventions ;
> Here no secret dark committee
> Spreads corruption through the city ;
> No place-men or pensioners here are haranguing ;
> No soldiers are shooting, or sailors are hanging ;
> No mutiny reigns in the army or fleet—
> For our orders are just, our commander discreet."

In imitation of the order of knighthood founded by the
government, the king of Dalkey founded the order of Druids.
The president was furnished with a large medallion, representing the bust of one of those mysterious persons, which he wore
on state occasions suspended from his neck.

Among the persons who took part in the convivialities of the kingdom of Dalkey, was the celebrated T. O'Meara, As the times became menacing, and Ireland infected with French principles, the Lord Chancellor Clare was vigilant in watching every society which was formed, and, among the rest, the kingdom of Dalkey and its Druids attracted his notice. O'Meara was personally known to him, and supposing he could enlighten him, Lord Clare sent for him.

"You, sir," said the chancellor, " are, I understand, connected with the kingdom of Dalkey."

"I am, my lord," said O'Meara.

"Pray, may I ask what title are you recognised by ?"

"I am Duke of Muglins."

"And what post do you hold under the government ?"

"Chief Commissioner of the Revenue."

"What are your emoluments in right of your office ?"

"I am allowed to import ten thousand hogsheads, duty free."

"Hogsheads of what, Mr. Commissioner ?"

"Of salt water, my lord."

The chancellor was satisfied without further question.

T. O'Meara was an attorney well known at that time, as many of the same profession were, for his conviviality, spirit wit, singularity, and good nature. Among other anecdotes told of him was one very characteristic. An Englishman of rank and fortune visited Ireland, and accidentally met him at dinner at a friend's house. It was then the hospitable custom for every person who met a stranger at a friend's house to ask him to dinner, and show him every attention. This was done with more than usual attention by O'Meara, who attached himself to the Englishman, invited him to his house in the country, and in the display of his good nature and sense of hospitality, gave up his time and business to make the visit agreeable and instructive to his acquaintance, who left Ireland with many expressions of obligation, for the kindness and attention he had received. Soon after, O'Meara for the first time visited London, and being a total stranger there was well pleased to see one day his English acquaintance walking on the other side of Bond Street; so he immediately crossed over, and with outstretched hand declared how delighted he was to see him again. The gentleman was walking with a group of others of a high aristocratic cast, and dressed in the utmost propriety of costume; and when he saw a wild-looking man, with soiled leather breeches, dirty top-boots, not over clean linen, nor very close shaven beard, striding up to him, with a whip in his hand and the lash twisted under his arm, he started back, and with a look of cold surprise said—

" Sir, you have the advantage of me."

"I have sir," said O'Meara, looking coolly at him for a moment—" I have, sir, and by —— I'll keep it;" and turned from him, casting such a look of contempt and superiority, as the other did not think it prudent to notice.

The last anniversary of the kingdom of Dalkey was, as we have mentioned, held in August, 1797.

The concourse of spectators on the shore and island on that occasion was estimated at not less than twenty thousand. The popular interest excited by the proceedings of the society and its free political sentiments were considered dangerous in the then excited state of the public mind; and to avoid being suppressed by the strong arm of the government, its meetings were, during the disturbed and alarming crisis of 1798, discontinued, and were never revived.

BOOKS OF IRISH INTEREST
FROM IRISH ACADEMIC PRESS

Birmingham, George A. **The Red Hand of Ulster**
(1912) A novel set in the Ulster of 1912, dominated
by fierce party strife over the Home Rule issue
and the prospect of armed rebellion 298pp

Byrne, Miles **Memoirs of Miles Byrne** (1863) Account
of experiences in rebellions of 1798 and 1803 3 vols
in 1 1000pp

Cosgrave, Dillon **North Dublin: City and County**
(1909) A Four Courts Press edition; surveys history,
conditions, customs and characters 138pp

Daunt, W.J. O'Neill **A Life Spent for Ireland** (1896)
Firsthand journals of nineteenth-century Irish revolutionary 440pp

BOOKS OF IRISH INTEREST
FROM IRISH ACADEMIC PRESS

Deane, Seamus **Gradual Wars** (1972) A new impression of AE Award-winning collection of poems that explore the complex nature of language, love and violence in the world today 64pp

Denieffe, Joseph **A Personal Narrative of the Irish Revolutionary Brotherhood** (1906) introduced by Sean O Luing. A good source for Fenian history in Ireland and America 324pp

Denvir, John **The Life Story of an Old Rebel** (1910) Activities of Irish republicans in Britain in the nineteenth century 306pp

Devoy, John **Recollections of an Irish Rebel** (1929), introduced by Sean O Luing. Devoy's life spanned that of the Fenian movement 508pp

BOOKS OF IRISH INTEREST
FROM IRISH ACADEMIC PRESS

Hyde, Douglas **Beside the Fire** (1910) A dual language collection of folk-tales with a long review of previous work on Irish folklore 254pp

Larminie, William **West Irish Folk-Tales and Romances** (1893) Eighteen stories collected around 1885 from peasants in Galway, Mayo and Donegal 286pp

MacLysaght, Edward **The Surnames of Ireland** (1978) The third edition, listing more than 4000 Gaelic, Norman and Anglo-Irish surnames and giving a wealth of information on the background of Irish families; by the leading authority on the subject 404pp

Teeling, Charles Hamilton **History of the Irish Rebellion of 1798, and Sequel** (1876) Account by a journalist who was also a United Irishman 384pp

OTHER BOOKS
FROM
FOUR COURTS PRESS

Michael Adams
SINGLE-MINDED

Deals with sexuality, and chastity as a virtue;
the purpose of celibacy and its location among
ordinary Christians; and difficulties experienced
by those who have accepted the charism of celibacy.

Salvatore Canals
JESUS AS FRIEND

A series of meditations on Christian living,
translated from Italian.

Newman, Jeremiah, **The State of Ireland**
The Bishop of Limerick deals with Church-State
and socio-moral questions in this Four Courts Press
book.